Web Programming For Beginners: Mastering HTML,DHTML,XHTML And JavaScript

Anshuman Mishra

Published by Anshuman Mishra, 2025.

ABOUT THE BOOK:

WEB PROGRAMMING FOR BEGINNERS: MASTERING HTML, DHTML, XHTML, AND JAVASCRIPT IS A COMPREHENSIVE GUIDE DESIGNED TO INTRODUCE STUDENTS AND BEGINNERS TO THE WORLD OF WEB DEVELOPMENT. THIS BOOK COVERS THE ESSENTIAL TECHNOLOGIES REQUIRED TO CREATE DYNAMIC AND INTERACTIVE WEB PAGES, INCLUDING HTML, XHTML, DHTML, AND JAVASCRIPT. WHETHER YOU'RE CREATING YOUR FIRST WEBSITE OR LOOKING TO EXPAND YOUR KNOWLEDGE OF WEB PROGRAMMING, THIS BOOK PROVIDES YOU WITH A SOLID FOUNDATION.

THE BOOK STARTS WITH THE BASICS, EXPLAINING WHAT WEB DEVELOPMENT IS AND HOW TO STRUCTURE YOUR WEB PAGES WITH HTML. IT THEN MOVES INTO MORE ADVANCED TOPICS LIKE XHTML FOR WELL-FORMED CODE AND DHTML TO ADD INTERACTIVITY AND DYNAMIC FEATURES TO YOUR WEB PAGES. THE FINAL SECTIONS FOCUS ON JAVASCRIPT, TEACHING YOU HOW TO BRING YOUR PAGES TO LIFE BY RESPONDING TO USER ACTIONS, PERFORMING CALCULATIONS, AND MANIPULATING PAGE CONTENT.

THROUGH PRACTICAL EXAMPLES, EASY-TO-FOLLOW INSTRUCTIONS, AND CLEAR EXPLANATIONS, THIS BOOK ENSURES THAT READERS CAN GRADUALLY BUILD THEIR WEB DEVELOPMENT SKILLS WHILE WORKING ON REAL-WORLD PROJECTS.

ADVANTAGES OF READING THIS BOOK:

1. **BEGINNER-FRIENDLY APPROACH**: THIS BOOK IS DESIGNED WITH BEGINNERS IN MIND, BREAKING DOWN COMPLEX CONCEPTS INTO SIMPLE AND EASY-TO-UNDERSTAND EXPLANATIONS. EVEN IF YOU'RE ENTIRELY NEW TO PROGRAMMING, YOU'LL FIND IT EASY TO FOLLOW THE STEP-BY-STEP INSTRUCTIONS.
2. **COMPREHENSIVE COVERAGE**: UNLIKE OTHER INTRODUCTORY BOOKS THAT FOCUS ON JUST ONE TECHNOLOGY, THIS BOOK COVERS HTML, XHTML, DHTML, AND JAVASCRIPT IN ONE PACKAGE, GIVING YOU A BROAD UNDERSTANDING OF WEB PROGRAMMING AND HOW DIFFERENT TECHNOLOGIES INTERACT WITH EACH OTHER.
3. **HANDS-ON LEARNING**: THE BOOK EMPHASIZES PRACTICAL LEARNING WITH REAL-WORLD EXAMPLES AND EXERCISES AT THE END OF EACH CHAPTER. YOU'LL BUILD ACTUAL WEB PAGES AND FEATURES AS YOU PROGRESS, WHICH WILL HELP YOU SOLIDIFY YOUR UNDERSTANDING.

4. **BUILD DYNAMIC WEBSITES**: AFTER READING THIS BOOK, YOU'LL HAVE THE SKILLS TO CREATE NOT JUST STATIC WEB PAGES BUT ALSO DYNAMIC AND INTERACTIVE WEBSITES USING JAVASCRIPT AND DHTML. YOU WILL LEARN HOW TO ADD INTERACTIVITY, CREATE RESPONSIVE DESIGNS, AND HANDLE USER INPUTS.

5. **UP-TO-DATE INFORMATION**: THE BOOK OFFERS UPDATED CONTENT ON WEB DEVELOPMENT STANDARDS AND BEST PRACTICES, INCLUDING THE USE OF XHTML FOR WELL-FORMED DOCUMENTS AND JAVASCRIPT LIBRARIES THAT CAN ENHANCE YOUR PROJECTS.

6. **FOCUS ON WEB STANDARDS AND ACCESSIBILITY**: THIS BOOK STRESSES THE IMPORTANCE OF WRITING CLEAN, VALID CODE THAT ADHERES TO WEB STANDARDS AND ACCESSIBILITY PRINCIPLES, MAKING SURE YOUR WEBSITES ARE ACCESSIBLE TO ALL USERS, INCLUDING THOSE WITH DISABILITIES.

HOW TO READ THIS BOOK:

1. **START FROM THE BEGINNING**: BEGIN BY READING CHAPTER 1, WHICH INTRODUCES THE BASICS OF WEB PROGRAMMING. EACH CHAPTER BUILDS ON THE PREVIOUS ONE, SO IT'S IMPORTANT TO GO THROUGH THE MATERIAL IN ORDER.

2. **WORK THROUGH PRACTICAL EXAMPLES**: AS YOU READ EACH CHAPTER, TAKE THE TIME TO WORK THROUGH THE EXAMPLES. THIS HANDS-ON APPROACH WILL HELP YOU UNDERSTAND HOW TO APPLY THE CONCEPTS IN REAL-WORLD SCENARIOS.

3. **TRY THE EXERCISES**: AT THE END OF EACH CHAPTER, YOU'LL FIND EXERCISES THAT TEST YOUR KNOWLEDGE AND HELP REINFORCE WHAT YOU'VE LEARNED. MAKE SURE TO COMPLETE THESE EXERCISES TO PRACTICE YOUR SKILLS AND IDENTIFY AREAS WHERE YOU MAY NEED TO REVIEW THE MATERIAL.

4. **USE THE INTERNET FOR ADDITIONAL LEARNING**: DON'T HESITATE TO LOOK UP ADDITIONAL RESOURCES, TUTORIALS, OR DOCUMENTATION ONLINE IF YOU ENCOUNTER A CONCEPT YOU'D LIKE TO EXPLORE FURTHER. THE BOOK PROVIDES A STRONG FOUNDATION, BUT THE WEB IS A VAST RESOURCE WHERE YOU CAN EXPAND YOUR KNOWLEDGE.

5. **EXPERIMENT WITH YOUR OWN PROJECTS**: AS YOU PROGRESS THROUGH THE BOOK, START WORKING ON YOUR OWN WEB PROJECTS. APPLY THE SKILLS YOU'VE LEARNED TO CREATE PERSONAL WEBSITES, BLOGS, OR OTHER SMALL PROJECTS. EXPERIMENTING WITH YOUR OWN IDEAS WILL HELP YOU DEVELOP DEEPER INSIGHTS INTO WEB PROGRAMMING.

6. **REFER BACK AS NEEDED**: DON'T FEEL LIKE YOU NEED TO MEMORIZE EVERYTHING AT ONCE. THE BOOK IS DESIGNED TO BE A REFERENCE GUIDE AS WELL. IF YOU FORGET A CONCEPT OR NEED CLARIFICATION, FEEL FREE TO REVISIT PREVIOUS CHAPTERS AND EXAMPLES.

7. **PRACTICE REGULARLY**: LIKE ANY PROGRAMMING SKILL, WEB DEVELOPMENT IMPROVES WITH PRACTICE. TRY TO CODE REGULARLY, BUILD PROJECTS, AND CONTINUALLY CHALLENGE YOURSELF WITH NEW TECHNIQUES AS YOU PROGRESS THROUGH THE BOOK.

TITLE: *WEB PROGRAMMING FOR BEGINNERS: MASTERING HTML, DHTML, XHTML, AND JAVASCRIPT*

CONTENT OVERVIEW:

ABOUT THE AUTHOR

ANSHUMAN MISHRA, AN ACCOMPLISHED ACADEMIC AND EDUCATOR, HAS OVER 18 YEARS OF TEACHING EXPERIENCE AS AN ASSISTANT PROFESSOR IN COMPUTER SCIENCE. HE HOLDS AN M.TECH IN COMPUTER SCIENCE FROM THE PRESTIGIOUS BIRLA INSTITUTE OF TECHNOLOGY, MESRA. CURRENTLY SERVING AT DORANDA COLLEGE, RANCHI, HE SPECIALIZES IN PROGRAMMING LANGUAGES, SOFTWARE DEVELOPMENT, AND COMPUTER SKILLS, INSPIRING COUNTLESS STUDENTS WITH HIS PROFOUND KNOWLEDGE AND PRACTICAL INSIGHTS.

ANSHUMAN IS A PASSIONATE WRITER WITH EXPERTISE IN CREATING EDUCATIONAL RESOURCES FOR STUDENTS AND PROFESSIONALS. HIS BOOKS COVER TOPICS LIKE JAVA PROGRAMMING, SQL, OPERATING SYSTEMS, AND COMPETITIVE PROGRAMMING, REFLECTING HIS DEDICATION TO MAKING COMPLEX SUBJECTS ACCESSIBLE AND ENGAGING.

BEYOND ACADEMICS, ANSHUMAN IS A MOTIVATIONAL THINKER, A LOVER OF MYSTERIES, AND A STORYTELLER AT HEART. HE HAS AUTHORED WORKS RANGING FROM SELF-MOTIVATION GUIDES TO CHILDREN'S STORIES AND BOOKS DELVING INTO THE RICH HISTORY AND CULTURE OF JHARKHAND. HIS ABILITY TO WEAVE KNOWLEDGE WITH INSPIRATION MAKES HIS BOOKS A TREASURE FOR READERS OF ALL AGES.

"Programs must be written for people to read, and only incidentally for machines to execute."
— Harold Abelson & Gerald Jay Sussman, *Structure and Interpretation of Computer Programs*

Copyright Page

Title: *WEB PROGRAMMING FOR BEGINNERS: MASTERING HTML, DHTML, XHTML, AND JAVASCRIPT*

Author: Anshuman Kumar Mishra
Copyright © 2025 by Anshuman Kumar Mishra

This book is published for educational purposes and is intended to serve as a comprehensive guide for MCA and BCA students, educators, and aspiring programmers. The author has made every effort to ensure accuracy, but neither the author nor the publisher assumes responsibility for errors, omissions, or any consequences arising from the application of information in this book.

INTRODUCTION TO WEB PROGRAMMING

What is Web Programming?

Web programming refers to the process of designing, developing, and maintaining websites, web applications, and web-based services. It involves the use of various programming languages, tools, and technologies to create the structure, behavior, and functionality of web pages and online platforms that users access through web browsers on the internet.

At its core, web programming ensures that a website or web application is interactive, responsive, and user-friendly, while also handling the back-end operations such as data processing, storage, and interaction with other services or databases. Web programming covers a broad range of tasks, from building the layout and design of a website (front-end development) to managing how a website functions and processes data behind the scenes (back-end development).

Web programming is essential for the creation of websites, e-commerce platforms, social media applications, content management systems (CMS), and many other online services. It combines creativity (design and user experience) with technical skills (code and logic) to provide a seamless web experience.

Two Main Areas of Web Programming

Web programming is typically divided into two primary areas:

1. **Front-End Development (Client-Side)**

   Front-end development focuses on what the user interacts with directly in their web browser. It involves the visual and interactive aspects of a website or application, and it is primarily concerned with how the website looks and how users experience it. Front-end developers ensure that users can easily navigate a website and engage with its features.

   Key Components of Front-End Development:

   - **HTML (HyperText Markup Language):**
     HTML is the fundamental building block of web pages. It provides the **structure** of a webpage by using a series of tags and elements. HTML defines the various sections of a webpage, such as headings, paragraphs, images, links, tables, and forms. Without HTML, a webpage wouldn't have any content or structure.

     For example, this HTML code creates a simple webpage with a heading and a paragraph:

     ```
     <html>
     ```

```
<head>
  <title>My Web Page</title>
</head>
<body>
  <h1>Welcome to My Website</h1>
  <p>This is my first webpage!</p>
</body>
</html>
```

- **CSS (Cascading Style Sheets)**:
  CSS is used to **style** the content created by HTML. It defines the appearance and layout of the webpage, such as colors, fonts, spacing, and positioning. CSS is essential for creating a visually appealing and well-organized website. It also allows web developers to make websites **responsive**, meaning they can adjust automatically to different screen sizes (e.g., mobile devices, desktops).

  For example, the following CSS code styles the text and background color of a webpage:

  ```
  body {
    font-family: Arial, sans-serif;
    background-color: #f4f4f4;
  }

  h1 {
    color: #333;
  }

  p {
    font-size: 16px;
  }
  ```

- **JavaScript**:
  JavaScript is a **programming language** that enables interactivity on a webpage. It allows for dynamic behavior, such as animations, interactive forms, pop-up messages, and real-time updates. JavaScript is used to respond to user actions, such as clicks, mouse movements, or keyboard inputs. It can also be used to manipulate HTML and CSS elements after the page has loaded, which is crucial for creating interactive web applications.

  For example, this JavaScript code changes the content of a paragraph when a user clicks a button:

  ```
  <button onclick="changeText()">Click Me!</button>
  <p id="demo">Hello, World!</p>

  <script>
    function changeText() {
      document.getElementById("demo").innerHTML = "You clicked the
  button!";
    }
  </script>
  ```

Front-End Frameworks & Libraries:

- **Frameworks**: Frameworks like **React**, **Angular**, and **Vue.js** help developers build complex and dynamic user interfaces more efficiently. These frameworks allow developers to create components that are reusable, maintainable, and can dynamically update the page based on user input or changes in the data.
- **Libraries**: Libraries like **jQuery** and **Bootstrap** provide pre-written code and UI components (e.g., buttons, navigation bars) that simplify front-end development.

2. **Back-End Development (Server-Side)**

Back-end development deals with the **server**, **database**, and the **application logic** that run behind the scenes of a website or application. It involves managing how the website communicates with the database, processes requests from users, and generates the necessary responses to send back to the client (front-end). The back-end is responsible for handling data, authenticating users, and ensuring that the application works correctly.

Key Components of Back-End Development:

- **Server-Side Programming Languages**: The back-end is built using server-side programming languages that process requests from the client and send back the appropriate response. Some popular server-side languages include:
  - **Python** (with frameworks like Django and Flask)
  - **PHP** (with frameworks like Laravel)
  - **Ruby** (with the Ruby on Rails framework)
  - **Java** (with frameworks like Spring)
  - **Node.js** (a JavaScript runtime for server-side development)

  These languages handle tasks such as routing (directing user requests to specific parts of the server), processing data, and generating dynamic content.

- **Databases**: A database stores the data that the website or application needs to function. For example, user information, product listings, comments, or transactions. There are two main types of databases used in web development:
  - **Relational Databases**: Use structured query language (SQL) to store data in tables. Examples include **MySQL**, **PostgreSQL**, and **SQLite**.
  - **NoSQL Databases**: Used for more flexible or large-scale data storage. Examples include **MongoDB**, **Cassandra**, and **CouchDB**.
- **Server-Side Frameworks**: Frameworks provide pre-built tools and libraries to help developers quickly build and deploy web applications. These frameworks provide solutions for common tasks such as routing, authentication, and database management. Examples of popular back-end frameworks include:
  - **Node.js** (JavaScript runtime for building scalable server-side applications)
  - **Django** (Python-based framework for rapid development)
  - **Flask** (Lightweight Python framework)
  - **Ruby on Rails** (A convention-over-configuration framework for Ruby)

- o **APIs (Application Programming Interfaces)**: APIs enable communication between the front-end and back-end. They allow data to be exchanged between the client and server, often in the form of JSON (JavaScript Object Notation) or XML.
  - **RESTful APIs**: Representational State Transfer (REST) is a widely used architectural style for building APIs. RESTful APIs define the set of rules for how clients (front-end) interact with the server and perform actions like retrieving, creating, or updating data.
  - **GraphQL**: An alternative to REST, GraphQL allows clients to request specific pieces of data, making it more efficient in some use cases.

Combining Front-End and Back-End for a Complete Web Application

Web programming combines both **front-end** and **back-end** development to create fully functional web applications. The front-end is responsible for presenting the content to users, while the back-end manages data processing and serves content to the front-end.

For example:

- A user fills out a form on a webpage (front-end).
- The form sends the data to the server for processing (back-end).
- The back-end saves the data to a database and sends a response to the front-end.
- The front-end then updates the webpage to show the result (e.g., a success message or a newly added entry).

Overview of Web Development Tools and Technologies

Web development involves a combination of various tools, technologies, and practices to build, design, and deploy websites and applications. The primary goal of web development is to create a seamless and engaging user experience, which requires a strong understanding of both front-end (client-side) and back-end (server-side) technologies. Below is a detailed overview of the main tools and technologies used in web development, organized by their roles in the development process.

1. Front-End Technologies

Front-end development refers to everything users interact with directly in their web browsers. It involves the design, layout, and functionality that users experience when they visit a website.

HTML (HyperText Markup Language)

HTML is the foundation of every webpage. It provides the basic structure for all web content such as headings, paragraphs, links, images, tables, and forms. HTML elements define how the content is displayed on a webpage and give it a hierarchical structure.

- Example:

```html
<html>
  <head>
    <title>Welcome to My Website</title>
  </head>
  <body>
    <h1>Welcome!</h1>
    <p>This is my first website.</p>
  </body>
</html>
```

CSS (Cascading Style Sheets)

CSS is used to style HTML elements by defining their layout, fonts, colors, margins, padding, and positioning. It enhances the visual appeal of a webpage and is critical for making a site responsive across different devices (mobile, tablet, desktop). CSS frameworks like Bootstrap and Tailwind CSS help streamline the design process by offering pre-built styles and components.

- Example:

```css
body {
  background-color: #f0f0f0;
  font-family: Arial, sans-serif;
}

h1 {
  color: #333;
}
```

JavaScript

JavaScript is a scripting language that enables interactivity on web pages. It allows dynamic behavior such as form validation, animations, content updates without reloading the page, and event handling like clicks, keypresses, and mouse movements.

- Example:

```html
<button onclick="alert('Hello, World!')">Click Me!</button>
```

CSS Frameworks (e.g., Bootstrap, Tailwind CSS)

CSS frameworks like **Bootstrap** and **Tailwind CSS** provide a collection of pre-designed, reusable UI components and styles that speed up development. These frameworks come with a grid system, typography, buttons, and other components that make web design faster and easier.

- **Bootstrap**: A widely used front-end framework for building responsive and mobile-first websites.
- **Tailwind CSS**: A utility-first CSS framework that allows developers to build custom designs quickly by composing utility classes.

JavaScript Libraries and Frameworks (e.g., jQuery, React, Angular, Vue.js)

JavaScript libraries and frameworks help developers create dynamic, interactive web applications with less effort and more consistency. These tools simplify tasks such as DOM manipulation, state management, and UI rendering.

- **jQuery**: A fast, small, and feature-rich JavaScript library. It simplifies event handling, AJAX requests, and DOM manipulation.
- **React**: A JavaScript library for building user interfaces, particularly single-page applications (SPAs), with reusable components.
- **Angular**: A full-fledged front-end framework for building complex web applications, developed by Google.
- **Vue.js**: A progressive JavaScript framework for building user interfaces. It is lightweight, flexible, and easy to integrate with other libraries.

---

2. Back-End Technologies

Back-end development involves the server-side of a website or application. It deals with the server, databases, and the logic behind processing user requests and delivering responses.

Programming Languages (e.g., Python, PHP, Java, Ruby, Node.js)

Back-end development uses programming languages to define the business logic and functionality of the application. These languages handle tasks like managing user authentication, querying databases, and generating dynamic content.

- **Python**: A versatile and beginner-friendly language, often used with frameworks like **Django** and **Flask** for web development.
- **PHP**: A server-side scripting language widely used for web development, especially with content management systems like WordPress.
- **Java**: A robust, object-oriented language used in enterprise-level web applications, commonly with frameworks like **Spring**.
- **Ruby**: Known for its simplicity and productivity, Ruby is often used with the **Ruby on Rails** framework for building web applications.

- **Node.js**: A JavaScript runtime built on Chrome's V8 engine that allows developers to write server-side code in JavaScript, commonly used with frameworks like **Express.js**.

Databases (e.g., MySQL, PostgreSQL, MongoDB)

Databases store and manage the data that a web application uses. There are two types of databases: relational (SQL) and non-relational (NoSQL).

- **MySQL**: A widely used relational database management system (RDBMS) that uses SQL to manage data.
- **PostgreSQL**: An advanced open-source RDBMS that emphasizes extensibility and SQL compliance.
- **MongoDB**: A NoSQL database that stores data in a flexible, document-based format (JSON-like). It is ideal for handling large amounts of unstructured data.

Server-Side Frameworks (e.g., Node.js, Django, Flask)

Back-end frameworks help developers build web applications more efficiently by providing tools, libraries, and predefined code structures.

- **Node.js**: As a runtime environment for JavaScript, Node.js also serves as a back-end framework that is highly scalable for building real-time applications.
- **Django**: A high-level Python web framework that encourages rapid development and clean, pragmatic design. It follows the "batteries-included" philosophy.
- **Flask**: A lightweight Python framework that is flexible and simple, allowing developers to build web applications with minimal overhead.

APIs (RESTful APIs / GraphQL)

APIs (Application Programming Interfaces) enable communication between the client-side (front-end) and server-side (back-end). They allow data to be exchanged between the front-end and the back-end, often in the form of JSON or XML.

- **RESTful APIs**: Representational State Transfer (REST) is an architectural style for creating web services. RESTful APIs are stateless and provide methods like GET, POST, PUT, and DELETE for interacting with resources.
- **GraphQL**: A query language for APIs that allows clients to request only the data they need, improving performance and flexibility.

3. Development Tools

These tools assist developers in writing, debugging, and managing code during the development process.

Text Editors/IDEs (e.g., Visual Studio Code, Sublime Text, Atom)

Text editors and Integrated Development Environments (IDEs) are used to write and edit code. IDEs often come with additional features like code completion, syntax highlighting, and debugging tools.

- **Visual Studio Code**: A powerful and widely used free code editor with rich extensions for web development.
- **Sublime Text**: A lightweight, fast text editor with a user-friendly interface and excellent support for plugins.
- **Atom**: An open-source text editor developed by GitHub, designed to be highly customizable.

Version Control Systems (e.g., Git)

Version control allows developers to track changes to their codebase over time and collaborate with other developers. It enables features like branching, merging, and reverting code changes.

- **Git**: The most widely used version control system that helps developers manage their source code history.
- **GitHub / GitLab**: Platforms that host Git repositories online and provide collaborative features like pull requests, issue tracking, and continuous integration.

Build Tools (e.g., Webpack, Gulp, Grunt)

Build tools help automate tasks like minifying JavaScript, compiling Sass to CSS, bundling modules, and optimizing images for faster load times.

- **Webpack**: A powerful module bundler that bundles JavaScript, CSS, and other assets into static files for production.
- **Gulp / Grunt**: Task runners that automate repetitive tasks like minification, transpilation, and file watching.

Browser Developer Tools (e.g., Chrome DevTools)

Most modern browsers include developer tools that allow developers to inspect and debug HTML, CSS, and JavaScript on live websites. These tools help identify performance issues, test responsiveness, and debug code.

- **Chrome DevTools**: The developer tools built into Google Chrome, offering features like element inspection, JavaScript debugging, network monitoring, and performance profiling.

4. Web Servers and Hosting

Once a web application is built, it needs to be hosted on a server so that users can access it via the internet.

Web Servers (e.g., Apache, Nginx)

Web servers handle incoming HTTP requests and serve web pages to users. They are essential for delivering content like HTML, CSS, images, and JavaScript.

- **Apache**: A popular, open-source web server that is flexible and configurable.
- **Nginx**: A high-performance web server and reverse proxy server that is widely used for serving static content and load balancing.

Hosting Services (e.g., AWS, Heroku, Netlify)

Hosting services provide the infrastructure needed to deploy web applications to the internet. These platforms offer cloud-based solutions for scalability, storage, and management.

- **AWS (Amazon Web Services)**: A comprehensive cloud platform that offers scalable hosting, storage, and computing resources.
- **Heroku**: A platform-as-a-service (PaaS) that simplifies deployment and scaling for web applications.
- **Netlify**: A cloud platform for deploying static websites and serverless functions, focused on simplicity and speed.

Setting up the Development Environment

Setting up a proper development environment is crucial for web programming. It ensures that you have all the tools, technologies, and configurations required to build, test, and deploy web applications. This environment includes a code editor or IDE, a local web server, version control, a database, and various other development tools. Below is a step-by-step guide to setting up a complete development environment for web development:

---

1. Install a Code Editor/IDE

A code editor or Integrated Development Environment (IDE) is where you'll write and edit your code. It is essential to have a powerful, efficient, and feature-rich editor that helps with coding, debugging, and testing.

- **Visual Studio Code**:
  Visual Studio Code (VS Code) is one of the most popular and widely used code editors for web development. It is free, lightweight, and highly customizable. It offers a rich set of features such as:
  - Syntax highlighting for multiple programming languages (HTML, CSS, JavaScript, etc.).
  - Built-in Git support for version control.
  - A wide range of extensions and plugins (e.g., linters, debuggers, live preview tools).
  - Integrated terminal for running commands directly in the editor.
  - Powerful debugging tools for both client-side (JavaScript) and server-side (Node.js, Python, etc.) code.
- **Sublime Text**:
  Sublime Text is a lightweight, fast, and responsive text editor that's ideal for simple web development tasks. It offers features like syntax highlighting, multi-caret editing, and customization, but may lack some of the more advanced features of an IDE.
- **Atom**:
  Atom is an open-source, user-friendly text editor developed by GitHub. It is known for its flexibility and customizable interface. Like Sublime Text, it supports a wide range of plugins and extensions for web development.

Installation:

- Download and install your preferred code editor from their respective websites:
  - <u>Visual Studio Code</u>
  - <u>Sublime Text</u>
  - <u>Atom</u>

2. Install a Local Web Server (for Back-End Development)

For server-side web development, you need a local environment that mimics how your application will run in production. This typically involves setting up a web server to handle requests and run back-end code.

Common Local Server Environments:

- **XAMPP/WAMP** (for PHP Development):
  - XAMPP and WAMP are popular local server environments for PHP developers. They provide a bundle of tools, including Apache (web server), MySQL (database), and PHP. These tools allow you to run PHP applications and interact with a database on your local machine before deploying to production.
  - Download from XAMPP or <u>WAMP</u>.

- **Node.js** (for JavaScript Back-End Development):
    - If you're working with JavaScript on the server-side, install **Node.js**, which enables you to run JavaScript outside of the browser. It also includes npm (Node Package Manager) to manage libraries and frameworks.
    - To install Node.js, visit Node.js official website.
- **Django** (for Python Development):
    - **Django** is a popular Python framework that allows you to quickly set up and deploy web applications. It comes with a built-in server for development purposes.
    - To install Django, use Python's package manager `pip`:

    ```
    pip install Django
    ```

- **Flask** (for Python Development):
    - **Flask** is a lightweight Python framework for building web applications. It's great for smaller applications or microservices.
    - To install Flask, use `pip`:

    ```
    pip install Flask
    ```

---

3. Install Version Control (Git)

Version control is essential for tracking changes in your codebase, collaborating with others, and maintaining a history of your project. **Git** is the most widely used version control system, and **GitHub** (or GitLab, Bitbucket) is a platform for hosting Git repositories.

Steps to Set Up Git:

- **Install Git**:
  Download and install Git from the official website: Git Downloads.

  After installation, open your terminal or command prompt and verify the installation by running:

  ```
  git --version
  ```

- **Create a GitHub Account**:
  If you haven't already, create an account on GitHub (or GitLab, Bitbucket) to host your code remotely. Visit GitHub to sign up.
- **Set Up Git**:
  Configure your Git user name and email:

  ```
  git config --global user.name "Your Name"
  git config --global user.email "your_email@example.com"
  ```

- **Initialize a Git Repository**:
  Create a new project and initialize a Git repository in the project folder:

```
git init
```

4. Set Up a Database

For dynamic websites or web applications, you'll need a database to store data such as user information, content, and more. There are two main types of databases: relational (SQL) and non-relational (NoSQL).

Common Databases:

- **MySQL/PostgreSQL** (Relational Databases):
  These are popular relational database management systems (RDBMS) that store data in tables and support SQL for querying.
  - **MySQL**: MySQL Official Website
  - **PostgreSQL**: PostgreSQL Official Website
- **MongoDB** (NoSQL Database):
  MongoDB is a NoSQL database that stores data in flexible, JSON-like documents. It's ideal for handling large volumes of unstructured data.
  - **MongoDB**: MongoDB Official Website

Installation:

- **MySQL/PostgreSQL**: Follow the installation guides provided on their official websites.
- **MongoDB**: Install MongoDB from the official website and follow the setup instructions.

5. Set Up Development Tools

Several additional development tools help streamline your workflow, automate repetitive tasks, and manage dependencies.

Common Development Tools:

- **Node.js** (for JavaScript Development):
  Node.js is essential for running JavaScript on the server-side. After installing Node.js, you can use **npm** (Node Package Manager) to install and manage libraries and frameworks.

```
npm install <package-name>
```

- **Webpack, Gulp, or Grunt** (for Task Automation):
  These tools automate tasks like minification, bundling, transpiling, and asset management. They help streamline the front-end build process.
  - **Webpack**: Webpack Official Website

- ○ **Gulp**: Gulp Official Website
- ○ **Grunt**: Grunt Official Website

---

6. Use a Browser for Testing

Testing your web pages and applications in a web browser is crucial for ensuring that your project functions as expected. Modern browsers come with built-in developer tools for inspecting and debugging code.

Recommended Browsers:

- **Google Chrome**: Chrome's Developer Tools (DevTools) allow you to inspect HTML, CSS, and JavaScript, debug code, and monitor network activity. Chrome DevTools Documentation
- **Mozilla Firefox**: Firefox also offers powerful developer tools for debugging and optimizing web pages. Firefox Developer Tools
- **Microsoft Edge**: Edge offers a set of tools similar to Chrome and Firefox, including features like visual debugging and responsive design testing.

---

7. Test Locally Before Deployment

Before deploying your website or web application to a production server, it's essential to test it locally to ensure that everything works correctly.

Steps to Test Locally:

1. **Run the Local Server**: Start your local development server (e.g., Node.js, XAMPP, Django) and navigate to your application in the browser.
   - ○ For example, with **Node.js**, you can use the following command to start your server:

   ```
   node server.js
   ```

   - ○ For **PHP**, if using XAMPP, you can start the Apache server and visit `http://localhost` in your browser.
2. **Test Functionality**: Test both front-end (HTML, CSS, JavaScript) and back-end (server logic, database interaction) features to make sure everything is functioning as expected.
3. **Debugging**: Use browser developer tools to inspect elements, check for JavaScript errors, and analyze performance.

25 multiple-choice questions (MCQs):

What is Web Programming?

1. **What does web programming primarily focus on?**
   - o a) Managing network security
   - o b) Developing mobile applications
   - o c) Creating and managing websites and web applications
   - o d) Writing system-level software
   - o **Answer**: c) Creating and managing websites and web applications

2. **Which of the following is a client-side technology in web programming?**
   - o a) PHP
   - o b) HTML
   - o c) Java
   - o d) MySQL
   - o **Answer**: b) HTML

3. **Which language is mainly used for server-side programming in web development?**
   - o a) HTML
   - o b) JavaScript
   - o c) Python
   - o d) CSS
   - o **Answer**: c) Python

4. **Which of the following is NOT a key part of front-end development?**
   - o a) HTML
   - o b) CSS
   - o c) Node.js
   - o d) JavaScript
   - o **Answer**: c) Node.js

5. **Which of these technologies is used for creating interactive elements on web pages?**
   - o a) JavaScript
   - o b) HTML
   - o c) MySQL
   - o d) PHP
   - o **Answer**: a) JavaScript

6. **Which protocol is commonly used for communication between client and server in web development?**
   - o a) HTTP
   - o b) FTP
   - o c) POP3
   - o d) SSH
   - o **Answer**: a) HTTP

7. **Which of these languages is commonly used for server-side programming?**
   - o a) HTML
   - o b) CSS
   - o c) PHP

- o d) jQuery
- o **Answer**: c) PHP

8. **Which of the following is used to style the HTML elements on a webpage?**
   - o a) JavaScript
   - o b) CSS
   - o c) PHP
   - o d) SQL
   - o **Answer**: b) CSS

9. **Which of the following is a back-end technology for web development?**
   - o a) React
   - o b) Flask
   - o c) Bootstrap
   - o d) jQuery
   - o **Answer**: b) Flask

10. **What does the term "full-stack" web development refer to?**

- a) Working only on the back-end of a web application
- b) Working only on the front-end of a web application
- c) Developing both the front-end and back-end of a web application
- d) Managing web servers and databases
- **Answer**: c) Developing both the front-end and back-end of a web application

---

Overview of Web Development Tools and Technologies

11. **Which of the following is a CSS framework used to speed up web design?**

- a) Django
- b) React
- c) Bootstrap
- d) MongoDB
- **Answer**: c) Bootstrap

12. **What does JavaScript help with in web programming?**

- a) Creating database connections
- b) Making a webpage interactive
- c) Styling HTML elements
- d) Providing back-end logic
- **Answer**: b) Making a webpage interactive

13. **Which tool is used to manage code repositories in version control?**

- a) npm
- b) Git
- c) React

- d) Webpack
- **Answer**: b) Git

14. **Which of the following is a JavaScript library for building user interfaces?**

- a) Django
- b) React
- c) Flask
- d) Laravel
- **Answer**: b) React

15. **What is the primary function of a web server?**

- a) To store data
- b) To manage user sessions
- c) To serve web pages to users
- d) To manage network traffic
- **Answer**: c) To serve web pages to users

16. **Which of these is a popular relational database management system (RDBMS) for web development?**

- a) MongoDB
- b) PostgreSQL
- c) Redis
- d) Elasticsearch
- **Answer**: b) PostgreSQL

17. **Which development tool automates repetitive tasks such as minification and bundling?**

- a) Webpack
- b) Git
- c) Sublime Text
- d) React
- **Answer**: a) Webpack

18. **Which database is commonly used for NoSQL web applications?**

- a) MySQL
- b) MongoDB
- c) PostgreSQL
- d) SQLite
- **Answer**: b) MongoDB

19. **Which of the following is an example of a back-end web framework?**

- a) Angular

- b) Node.js
- c) Bootstrap
- d) Vue.js
- **Answer**: b) Node.js

20. **Which of the following tools is used for debugging and inspecting the behavior of a webpage?**

- a) Chrome DevTools
- b) Git
- c) MongoDB
- d) React
- **Answer**: a) Chrome DevTools

Setting up the Development Environment

21. **What is the first step to setting up a web development environment?**

- a) Install a database server
- b) Install a text editor or IDE
- c) Install version control
- d) Install a local server
- **Answer**: b) Install a text editor or IDE

22. **Which software is used for local web server environments for PHP development?**

- a) Node.js
- b) XAMPP
- c) Git
- d) Django
- **Answer**: b) XAMPP

23. **Which of the following tools is used for installing and managing JavaScript libraries and frameworks?**

- a) npm
- b) Git
- c) MySQL
- d) Webpack
- **Answer**: a) npm

24. **Which of the following is a common development environment for running Python-based web applications?**

- a) Flask
- b) Django

- c) Node.js
- d) Ruby on Rails
- **Answer**: b) Django

25. **What is the purpose of using Git in web development?**

- a) To manage project dependencies
- b) To serve web pages
- c) To track code changes and collaborate with others
- d) To debug JavaScript code
- **Answer**: c) To track code changes and collaborate with others

25 short questions and answers

What is Web Programming?

1. **Q: What is web programming?**
   - **A:** Web programming involves creating and developing websites and web applications using various technologies like HTML, CSS, JavaScript, and server-side programming languages.
2. **Q: What is the primary role of HTML in web development?**
   - **A:** HTML (HyperText Markup Language) provides the basic structure of a webpage, defining elements like headings, paragraphs, links, and images.
3. **Q: What does CSS stand for, and what is its purpose?**
   - **A:** CSS (Cascading Style Sheets) is used to define the presentation, style, and layout of web pages, such as colors, fonts, and positioning.
4. **Q: What is the purpose of JavaScript in web programming?**
   - **A:** JavaScript is used to add interactivity and dynamic behavior to web pages, such as handling form validation, animations, and user interactions.
5. **Q: What is the difference between front-end and back-end development?**
   - **A:** Front-end development focuses on the user interface and experience (HTML, CSS, JavaScript), while back-end development handles the server, databases, and application logic.
6. **Q: What is a web framework?**
   - **A:** A web framework provides pre-written code libraries and tools to help developers build web applications more efficiently, such as Django (Python), Ruby on Rails (Ruby), and Node.js (JavaScript).
7. **Q: What is the role of a server in web programming?**
   - **A:** The server processes client requests and serves web pages and resources, handling tasks like data storage and processing.

8. **Q: What does API stand for, and what is its role in web development?**
   - **A:** API (Application Programming Interface) allows communication between different software systems, enabling the front-end to interact with the back-end or external services.
9. **Q: What is a database in the context of web development?**
   - **A:** A database is used to store and manage data such as user information, content, or transactions for web applications.
10. **Q: What is the role of security in web programming?**
    - **A:** Security in web programming ensures that web applications are protected from attacks like SQL injection, cross-site scripting (XSS), and unauthorized access.

Overview of Web Development Tools and Technologies

11. **Q: What is the purpose of a code editor in web development?**
    - **A:** A code editor is used to write and edit source code for web applications. Examples include Visual Studio Code, Sublime Text, and Atom.
12. **Q: What is the role of version control in web development?**
    - **A:** Version control systems like Git help track changes in the codebase, manage code revisions, and collaborate with others.
13. **Q: What is a CSS framework, and give an example?**
    - **A:** A CSS framework is a pre-built collection of CSS styles to speed up web design. An example is Bootstrap.
14. **Q: What is the purpose of JavaScript libraries?**
    - **A:** JavaScript libraries simplify common programming tasks and improve code efficiency. Examples include jQuery, React, and Vue.js.
15. **Q: What is Node.js used for in web development?**
    - **A:** Node.js is a JavaScript runtime that allows developers to write server-side code using JavaScript, enabling full-stack development.
16. **Q: What is a relational database, and give an example?**
    - **A:** A relational database stores data in structured tables and uses SQL for queries. Examples include MySQL and PostgreSQL.
17. **Q: What is the difference between SQL and NoSQL databases?**
    - **A:** SQL databases are relational and use structured queries (e.g., MySQL), while NoSQL databases are non-relational and more flexible (e.g., MongoDB).
18. **Q: What is the purpose of a web server?**
    - **A:** A web server hosts and serves web pages to clients (users) by processing HTTP requests and sending back the appropriate response.
19. **Q: What does the term "full-stack development" mean?**
    - **A:** Full-stack development refers to the development of both the front-end (user interface) and back-end (server and database) of a web application.
20. **Q: What is the function of APIs in web development?**
    - **A:** APIs enable communication between different parts of an application or between different applications, such as connecting the front-end with the back-end.

Setting up the Development Environment

21. **Q: What is the first step in setting up a web development environment?**
    - o **A:** The first step is to install a code editor or IDE, such as Visual Studio Code, Sublime Text, or Atom.
22. **Q: What is the purpose of a local server in web development?**
    - o **A:** A local server simulates a production environment on your computer, allowing you to test web applications before deploying them live.
23. **Q: What is Git, and why is it important for web developers?**
    - o **A:** Git is a version control system that helps developers track code changes, collaborate with others, and manage different versions of their projects.
24. **Q: What are the common tools used for managing dependencies in JavaScript?**
    - o **A:** npm (Node Package Manager) and Yarn are commonly used tools for managing JavaScript libraries and dependencies.
25. **Q: Why is it important to test locally before deploying a web application?**
    - o **A:** Testing locally ensures that the application functions correctly, helps identify bugs, and prevents errors from affecting live users when deployed.

CHAPTER 1: UNDERSTANDING HTML (HYPERTEXT MARKUP LANGUAGE)

HTML (HyperText Markup Language) is the foundational language used for creating and designing web pages and web applications. It is a markup language, meaning it uses tags to structure and organize content on the web. HTML is responsible for providing the basic structure of web pages, including text, images, links, tables, and multimedia content.

HTML documents are interpreted by web browsers to display the content visually to users. While HTML provides the structure, other technologies like **CSS (Cascading Style Sheets)** are used to add style, and **JavaScript** is used for interactivity. Together, HTML, CSS, and JavaScript form the core of web development.

Basic Structure of an HTML Document

An HTML document consists of a series of nested elements, each serving a particular purpose. The following is the basic skeleton of an HTML document:

```
<!DOCTYPE html>
<html lang="en">
  <head>
    <meta charset="UTF-8">
    <meta name="viewport" content="width=device-width, initial-scale=1.0">
    <title>Document Title</title>
  </head>
  <body>
    <h1>Welcome to My Webpage</h1>
    <p>This is a paragraph of text.</p>
  </body>
</html>
```

Explanation of the HTML Structure:

1. **`<!DOCTYPE html>`**:
   - This declaration defines the document type and specifies the version of HTML being used. In this case, `<!DOCTYPE html>` indicates that the document is written in **HTML5**, the latest version of HTML.
   - It ensures that the document follows the HTML5 standard, helping the browser render the content appropriately.
2. **`<html lang="en">`**:
   - The `<html>` element is the root of the HTML document, which encapsulates all the content of the page.
   - The `lang="en"` attribute specifies that the primary language of the document is English. This is useful for accessibility tools like screen readers and helps search engines identify the language of the page.
3. **`<head>`**:
   - The `<head>` element contains metadata about the document, which is not displayed directly on the webpage but is essential for the document's proper functioning.

- It can include links to external resources like CSS files, JavaScript files, and font files, as well as important information like the document's title, character encoding, and viewport settings.

4. **`<meta charset="UTF-8">`:**
   - The `<meta>` tag with `charset="UTF-8"` specifies the character encoding used in the document. UTF-8 is a popular encoding that supports almost all characters from various languages.
   - This ensures that the text on the webpage is rendered correctly, including special characters, accents, and non-English characters.

5. **`<meta name="viewport" content="width=device-width, initial-scale=1.0">`:**
   - This meta tag is crucial for making a webpage responsive, meaning it will adapt to different screen sizes, especially on mobile devices.
   - The `width=device-width` setting ensures the webpage is scaled to fit the width of the device's screen.
   - The `initial-scale=1.0` specifies the initial zoom level when the page is loaded.

6. **`<title>`:**
   - The `<title>` tag defines the title of the web page, which is displayed in the browser tab. It's essential for both user navigation and search engine optimization (SEO).
   - The title should be descriptive and relevant to the content of the page.

7. **`<body>`:**
   - The `<body>` element contains all the visible content of the webpage that the user interacts with.
   - This is where headings, paragraphs, images, videos, links, and other content are placed to be displayed on the page.

In the example above:

- `<h1>Welcome to My Webpage</h1>` is a heading that gives the main title of the page, displayed in a large font by default.
- `<p>This is a paragraph of text.</p>` is a paragraph containing a brief description or content for the page.

Breaking Down the HTML Tags

- **`<html>`**: Encloses all HTML content on the page.
- **`<head>`**: Contains metadata that is not directly visible on the webpage, such as links to CSS files and the page title.
- **`<meta>`**: Provides meta-information like character encoding or viewport settings.
- **`<title>`**: Sets the title of the webpage that appears on the browser tab.
- **`<body>`**: Contains all the visible content of the page.
- **`<h1>`**: Represents the highest-level heading, typically used for the main title.
- **`<p>`**: Defines a paragraph of text.

1. of the webpage (headings, paragraphs, images, etc.).

Elements, Tags, and Attributes

In HTML, **elements**, **tags**, and **attributes** work together to structure and provide detailed information about content on a web page. Let's explore each of these concepts in detail.

---

1. Elements in HTML

An **element** is the basic building block of an HTML document. It consists of:

- A **start tag** (also called an opening tag)
- **Content** (optional)
- An **end tag** (also called a closing tag)

For example, the `<p>` element is used to define a paragraph in HTML. It contains content (text, images, other HTML elements) wrapped between an opening and closing tag.

Example:
```
<p>This is a paragraph.</p>
```

- **Start tag**: `<p>`
- **Content**: `This is a paragraph.`
- **End tag**: `</p>`

The content inside the element (`This is a paragraph.`) can be plain text, other elements, or multimedia, depending on the purpose of the element.

Types of Elements:

- **Empty or Self-closing elements**: These elements do not have an end tag. For example, the `<img>` element is self-closing, meaning it does not require a closing tag.

  ```
  <img src="image.jpg" alt="A beautiful landscape">
  ```

- **Block-level elements**: These elements generally start on a new line and take up the full width available (e.g., `<div>`, `<p>`, `<h1>`).
- **Inline elements**: These elements do not start on a new line and only take up as much width as necessary (e.g., `<span>`, `<a>`, `<strong>`).

---

2. Tags in HTML

Tags are special instructions or commands used to define elements in HTML. They are enclosed in angle brackets (`< >`) and are typically paired — with an opening tag and a closing tag.

- **Opening Tag**: This tag marks the beginning of an element. It usually contains the name of the element and may include attributes. For example, `<p>` is the opening tag for a paragraph.
- **Closing Tag**: This tag marks the end of the element. It is similar to the opening tag, but it includes a forward slash (/) before the element name. For example, `</p>` is the closing tag for a paragraph.

Example of a complete element:
```
<p>This is a paragraph.</p>
```

- **Opening tag**: `<p>`
- **Closing tag**: `</p>`

In HTML, most elements are wrapped in these paired tags, except for self-closing tags.

Important Tag Characteristics:

- Tags are case-insensitive in HTML, but it is a best practice to use lowercase for consistency and readability.
- Tags help the browser understand how to display the content and apply styles.

3. Attributes in HTML

Attributes provide additional information about an HTML element. They are always specified in the opening tag and consist of a **name** and a **value**. Attributes offer a way to configure the behavior, appearance, or characteristics of an element.

Syntax of an attribute:
```
<tagname attribute="value">content</tagname>
```

For example, in the `<img>` tag:

```
<img src="image.jpg" alt="A beautiful landscape" width="500">
```

- **src**: The source of the image (specifies the file location).
- **alt**: A text description of the image, which is shown if the image can't be loaded or for accessibility purposes (screen readers).
- **width**: Specifies the width of the image in pixels.

Key Points About Attributes:

1. **Attributes are always inside the opening tag** and provide additional functionality or information about the element.
2. **Attributes consist of a name and value**. The name specifies what kind of information you're providing, and the value describes that information.
3. **Attribute values are enclosed in quotes** (either single ' or double " quotes).

4. **Attributes are optional**, meaning not all elements require attributes, but they enhance the functionality and accessibility of the page.

Examples of Common HTML Attributes:

- **href**: Specifies the URL for a link (`<a>` tag).

  ```
  <a href="https://www.example.com">Visit Example</a>
  ```

- **src**: Specifies the source of an image or media file (`<img>`, `<audio>`, `<video>` **tags**).

  ```
  <img src="logo.png" alt="Company Logo">
  ```

- **class**: Used to assign a class to an element, which can be targeted by CSS or JavaScript.

  ```
  <div class="container">Content here</div>
  ```

- **id**: Provides a unique identifier for an element. It can be used for styling or JavaScript targeting.

  ```
  <h2 id="section1">Section 1</h2>
  ```

- **style**: Inline styles for the element, although it is often better to use external CSS files for styling.

  ```
  <p style="color:red;">This is a red paragraph.</p>
  ```

Self-closing Elements with Attributes:

Some HTML elements, such as `<img>`, `<input>`, `<br>`, and `<hr>`, are self-closing and do not require a closing tag. They can still contain attributes to define their properties.

Example:

```
<img src="picture.jpg" alt="Picture of a cat" width="300">
```

Here, the `<img>` element has the **src**, **alt**, and **width** attributes, but it doesn't have a closing tag.

Summary of Elements, Tags, and Attributes in HTML

1. **Elements**: An HTML element consists of a start tag, content, and an end tag. Elements define the structure and content of a webpage.
   - Example: `<p>This is a paragraph.</p>`
2. **Tags**: Tags are used to enclose elements in HTML. The start tag (`<p>`) marks the beginning of the element, and the end tag (`</p>`) marks the end of the element.
   - Example: `<p></p>`
3. **Attributes**: Attributes provide additional details about an element. They are defined within the start tag and consist of a name and a value.

      o   **Example:** `<img src="image.jpg" alt="Description" width="500">`

Common HTML Tags: Headings, Paragraphs, Links, Images, Forms

HTML provides several essential tags for structuring content on the web. These tags help in organizing and presenting text, links, images, and forms effectively. Let's explore some of the most common HTML tags in detail:

---

1. Headings: `<h1>` to `<h6>`

Headings are used to define the structure of the content, indicating sections and subsections. HTML provides six levels of headings, from `<h1>` to `<h6>`, where `<h1>` represents the highest (most important) level and `<h6>` is the lowest.

Example:
```
<h1>Main Heading</h1>
<h2>Subheading</h2>
<h3>Sub-subheading</h3>
```

- **`<h1>`**: The top-level heading. It's typically used for the main title of a webpage or a section.
- **`<h2>`**: Used for subsections under the `<h1>` heading.
- **`<h3>`, `<h4>`, `<h5>`, `<h6>`**: Further sublevels, used to organize the content hierarchically.

Purpose:

- Headings help with content organization and accessibility. They also play an important role in SEO (Search Engine Optimization) as search engines give more importance to `<h1>` content.

---

2. Paragraphs: `<p>`

The `<p>` tag is used to define a paragraph of text. It automatically adds space before and after the content, helping in the proper formatting of text on a webpage.

Example:
```
<p>This is a paragraph of text on a webpage.</p>
```

- **`<p>`**: Encloses a block of text, ensuring it's displayed as a distinct paragraph, separate from surrounding content.

Purpose:

- Paragraphs are crucial for displaying text content in a readable format. They provide separation between chunks of text, improving the overall organization and readability of the page.

3. Links: `<a>`

The `<a>` (anchor) tag is used to create hyperlinks, allowing users to navigate between different pages or websites. The `href` attribute specifies the destination URL.

Example:
```
<a href="https://www.example.com">Visit Example</a>
```

- **`href` attribute**: Specifies the URL the link will navigate to when clicked. This could be an internal or external link.
- **Link text**: The text between the opening and closing `<a>` tags will be clickable and serve as the hyperlink.

Purpose:

- Links are essential for navigation, connecting users to other web pages, resources, or external websites. They can also be used to trigger actions, such as opening an email or downloading a file.

4. Images: `<img>`

The `<img>` tag is used to display images on a webpage. It is a self-closing tag, meaning it does not require a closing tag. The `src` attribute specifies the image file's location, and the `alt` attribute provides alternative text that is displayed if the image cannot be loaded, or for users with screen readers.

Example:
```
<img src="image.jpg" alt="Description of the image">
```

- **`src`**: The **source** of the image file. It can be a local file path or an external URL.
- **`alt`**: The **alternative text** provides a description of the image, which is useful for accessibility and SEO. It's also shown when the image cannot be loaded.
- **Other optional attributes**: `width`, `height`, `title` (provides additional information when the user hovers over the image).

Purpose:

- The `<img>` tag is essential for embedding visual content into web pages. It ensures that users can view images and provides an alternative for those with accessibility needs.

5. Forms: `<form>`

Forms are used to gather user input. The `<form>` tag encloses form elements, which can include text fields, radio buttons, checkboxes, and submit buttons. Forms allow users to interact with the webpage, providing information that can be processed on the server.

Example:
```
<form action="/submit" method="POST">
  <label for="name">Name:</label>
  <input type="text" id="name" name="name">
  <input type="submit" value="Submit">
</form>
```

- **`<form>`**: The container for form elements. It uses the `action` attribute to specify where the form data should be sent for processing (usually to a server) and the `method` attribute to specify the HTTP method (typically GET or POST).
- **`<label>`**: Defines a label for an input element. The `for` attribute associates the label with a specific input element by its `id`.
- **`<input>`**: Defines different types of user input fields, such as text fields, checkboxes, or buttons. The `type` attribute specifies the type of input (e.g., `text`, `submit`, `radio`).
- **`<input type="submit">`**: Creates a submit button, which allows users to send the form data when clicked.

Purpose:

- Forms are essential for collecting data from users, such as names, emails, passwords, and preferences. They are commonly used in login pages, surveys, registrations, and e-commerce checkout systems.

Structuring Web Pages with Lists, Tables, and Forms

In HTML, lists, tables, and forms are key elements used to organize content, present data, and collect input from users. Below is an in-depth explanation of how to use each of these elements to structure web pages effectively:

---

1. Lists in HTML: `<ul>` and `<ol>`

HTML provides two main types of lists to organize information: **unordered lists** and **ordered lists**. Both are commonly used to display items in a specific sequence or without any order.

Unordered List (`<ul>`)

An unordered list is used when the order of list items does not matter. It typically displays items with bullet points.

Example:
```
<ul>
  <li>Item 1</li>
  <li>Item 2</li>
  <li>Item 3</li>
</ul>
```

- **<ul>**: The tag that defines an unordered list.
- **<li>**: Each item in the list is wrapped in an <li> tag. The items are displayed with bullet points by default.

Ordered List (<ol>)

An ordered list is used when the order of items is important. It typically displays items with numbered markers.

Example:
```
<ol>
  <li>First item</li>
  <li>Second item</li>
  <li>Third item</li>
</ol>
```

- **<ol>**: The tag that defines an ordered list.
- **<li>**: Each item in the list is wrapped in an <li> tag. The items are displayed with numbers by default.

List Usage:

- **Unordered lists** are often used for navigation menus, bullet points, or non-sequential lists.
- **Ordered lists** are commonly used for instructions, steps in a process, or ranked data.

You can also create **nested lists** (lists within lists) by placing <ul> or <ol> tags inside <li> tags, as shown in the example below:

```
<ol>
  <li>Step 1</li>
  <li>Step 2
    <ul>
      <li>Sub-step 2.1</li>
      <li>Sub-step 2.2</li>
    </ul>
  </li>
  <li>Step 3</li>
</ol>
```

2. Tables in HTML: `<table>`, `<tr>`, `<td>`, and `<th>`

Tables are used to display data in rows and columns. Tables are helpful for presenting structured information, such as spreadsheets, data comparisons, or tabular data. In HTML, you can define a table using the `<table>`, `<tr>`, `<td>`, and `<th>` tags.

Basic Structure of a Table:

```
<table>
  <tr>
    <th>Header 1</th>
    <th>Header 2</th>
  </tr>
  <tr>
    <td>Data 1</td>
    <td>Data 2</td>
  </tr>
  <tr>
    <td>Data 3</td>
    <td>Data 4</td>
  </tr>
</table>
```

- **`<table>`**: Defines the table element.
- **`<tr>`**: Defines a table row. A table can have multiple rows, each containing table data (`<td>`) or table headers (`<th>`).
- **`<th>`**: Defines a table header. It's typically displayed as bold and centered by default, and it's used to label the columns of the table.
- **`<td>`**: Defines table data. It contains the content for each cell in the table.

Example Explained:

- **First Row**: Contains two header cells (`<th>`), used to label the columns of the table.
- **Second and Third Rows**: Contain table data cells (`<td>`), which represent the actual data of the table.

Advanced Table Usage:

You can also add other attributes to improve the table's accessibility and readability, such as:

- **`colspan`**: Specifies how many columns a cell should span.
- **`rowspan`**: Specifies how many rows a cell should span.
- **Example with `colspan` and `rowspan`:**

```
<table>
  <tr>
    <th>Header 1</th>
    <th colspan="2">Header 2</th>
  </tr>
  <tr>
    <td rowspan="2">Rowspanned Data</td>
    <td>Data 1</td>
    <td>Data 2</td>
  </tr>
```

```
<tr>
  <td>Data 3</td>
  <td>Data 4</td>
</tr>
</table>
```

- In this example, the second header spans across two columns, and the first column spans across two rows.

---

3. Forms in HTML: `<form>`, `<input>`, `<label>`, and `<button>`

Forms are essential for collecting user input, such as text, selections, and submissions. In HTML, forms are defined with the `<form>` tag, and they can contain a variety of input fields, labels, and buttons.

Basic Form Structure:
```
<form action="/submit" method="POST">
  <label for="email">Email:</label>
  <input type="email" id="email" name="email" required>
  <input type="submit" value="Submit">
</form>
```

- **`<form>`**: The container for the form. It has two important attributes:
  - **`action`**: Specifies the URL where the form data will be sent for processing.
  - **`method`**: Defines how data is sent to the server. Common methods are GET (data sent in the URL) and POST (data sent in the body of the request).
- **`<label>`**: Defines a label for an input field. The `for` attribute associates the label with a specific input element using its `id`.
- **`<input>`**: The most commonly used element in a form. It defines different types of user input fields, such as:
  - **`type="text"`** for text input.
  - **`type="email"`** for email addresses.
  - **`type="password"`** for password fields.
  - **`type="submit"`** for a submit button.
- **`<button>`**: Defines a clickable button, which can trigger form submission or other actions.

Example Explained:

- The **`<label>`** is used for accessibility and tells the user what input is expected.
- The **`<input>`** allows users to enter data, such as an email address in the example above.
- The **`<input type="submit">`** creates a button that submits the form.

Additional Form Elements:

Forms can contain other input elements such as:

- **`<textarea>`**: For multi-line text input (e.g., a comment box).
- **`<select>`**: For dropdown menus.
- **`<option>`**: Defines the options inside a dropdown menu.
- **`<input type="radio">`**: For radio buttons (used for single-choice selections).
- **`<input type="checkbox">`**: For checkboxes (used for multiple-choice selections).

Example with More Input Types:

```
<form action="/submit" method="POST">
  <label for="username">Username:</label>
  <input type="text" id="username" name="username">

  <label for="gender">Gender:</label>
  <input type="radio" id="male" name="gender" value="Male"> Male
  <input type="radio" id="female" name="gender" value="Female"> Female

  <label for="preferences">Preferences:</label>
  <input type="checkbox" id="newsletter" name="newsletter" value="subscribe">
Subscribe to Newsletter

  <input type="submit" value="Submit">
</form>
```

- This example includes text inputs, radio buttons, checkboxes, and a submit button. It shows how forms can be customized to collect a variety of data.

Creating Links and Navigating Between Pages

Links are essential for navigation on the web. They allow users to move from one page to another, interact with different sections within a page, and access external resources. HTML provides the <a> (anchor) tag to create hyperlinks that enable this navigation.

1. Creating Links: The <a> Tag

The <a> tag is used to create hyperlinks, enabling users to navigate between pages, sites, or even specific sections of the same page. The key attribute for the <a> tag is the **href** (hypertext reference), which specifies the destination URL.

Example of a Basic Link:

```
<a href="page2.html">Go to Page 2</a>
```

- **`<a>`**: The anchor tag used to create a link.
- **`href="page2.html"`**: The **href** attribute specifies the location of the destination page. In this case, the link navigates to page2.html when clicked.
- **`Go to Page 2`**: The visible text that appears as a clickable link.

When users click on "Go to Page 2," their browser will load the `page2.html` file, provided it is in the same directory as the current page.

2. Linking to External Websites

In addition to linking to local files (like `page2.html`), the `<a>` tag is also commonly used to link to external websites. When linking to an external site, you specify the full URL (Uniform Resource Locator) of the destination in the **href** attribute.

Example of Linking to an External Website:
```
<a href="https://www.example.com" target="_blank">Visit Example Website</a>
```

- **href="https://www.example.com"**: The full URL specifies the external website to link to.
- **target="_blank"**: The **target** attribute determines where the linked document will open. In this case, the value **_blank** ensures the link opens in a new tab or window, leaving the current page intact. Without this attribute, the linked page would open in the same tab or window, replacing the current content.

When users click on the "Visit Example Website" link, it will open the **https://www.example.com** website in a new browser tab.

3. Navigating Within a Page (Anchor Links)

HTML allows links to navigate within the same page, rather than opening a new page. This is achieved using anchor links, where a link points to a specific section on the same page. To create this kind of navigation, you use the **id** attribute to mark the target section of the page.

Example of Navigating Within the Same Page:
```
<a href="#section1">Go to Section 1</a>

<!-- Section 1 -->
<div id="section1">
  <h2>Section 1</h2>
  <p>This is the content of Section 1.</p>
</div>
```

- **<a href="#section1">Go to Section 1</a>**: This link points to the element with the **id="section1"**. The **#** in the **href** attribute refers to the ID of the target section on the same page.
- **<div id="section1">**: The section that the link will navigate to when clicked. The **id="section1"** uniquely identifies this section, allowing the link to jump to this specific location on the page.

When a user clicks the link "Go to Section 1," the page will scroll to the part of the page where the `<div>` with the `id="section1"` exists.

Additional Attributes for Links

1. title Attribute:

The **title** attribute provides additional information when the user hovers over a link. This text will appear as a tooltip.

```
<a href="https://www.example.com" title="Click to visit Example
Website">Visit Example Website</a>
```

- **title="Click to visit Example Website"**: The **title** attribute gives users a hint or description of where the link will take them. This appears when the user hovers the mouse over the link.

2. rel Attribute:

The **rel** attribute specifies the relationship between the current document and the linked document. It is commonly used with external links for security purposes.

For example, when linking to an external website, using **rel="noopener noreferrer"** improves security by preventing the linked page from gaining access to the original page's `window` object.

```
<a href="https://www.example.com" target="_blank" rel="noopener
noreferrer">Visit Example Website</a>
```

- **rel="noopener noreferrer"**: Enhances security when opening links in a new tab. **noopener** prevents the new page from accessing the original page, and **noreferrer** prevents the browser from sending the referring page's URL to the destination site.

4. Opening Links in the Same Tab (Default Behavior)

By default, links open in the same tab or window unless specified otherwise with the **target="_blank"** attribute. If you do not use the `target` attribute, the link will replace the current content with the destination page.

```
<a href="https://www.example.com">Visit Example Website</a>
```

- This link will open **https://www.example.com** in the same tab.

5. Link Navigation with Query Parameters

Sometimes, links also pass information to the destination page using **query parameters** in the URL. These parameters are commonly used to pass data such as search queries or user IDs.

Example of Query Parameters in a Link:

```
<a href="search.html?query=HTML&category=web">Search for HTML Web
Articles</a>
```

- **search.html?query=HTML&category=web**: The URL has two query parameters: `query=HTML` and `category=web`. When the user clicks the link, the page can process these parameters to display relevant content.

Best Practices for Links

When working with HTML, links play a critical role in navigation and user experience. Following best practices ensures that links are both user-friendly and accessible. Below are detailed best practices for creating effective and accessible links:

---

1. Use Descriptive Anchor Text

The anchor text (the clickable text inside the `<a>` tag) is crucial for both usability and search engine optimization (SEO). It should clearly describe the content or action that will occur when the link is clicked.

- **Avoid Generic Text**: Phrases like "Click here" or "Read more" do not provide enough context and may confuse users, especially those using screen readers.
- **Use Specific and Contextual Text**: The anchor text should describe the destination or action the user will take by clicking the link. For example:
  - **Bad Example:** `<a href="https://example.com">Click here</a>`
  - **Good Example:** `<a href="https://example.com">Visit the Example Website for More Info</a>`

Descriptive anchor text not only helps users understand what they will be accessing but also contributes positively to SEO by signaling the relevance of the link's destination.

2. Consider Accessibility

Links must be accessible to all users, including those with disabilities. This means ensuring that users can navigate through links with a keyboard, and screen readers can properly interpret the link's purpose.

- **Keyboard Navigation**: Ensure that all interactive elements, including links, can be accessed using the keyboard alone. This is crucial for users who cannot use a mouse.
- **Screen Reader Friendly**: Use clear, descriptive text for links. Also, consider adding additional context with the `title` attribute, which provides supplementary information when the user hovers over the link.

```
<a href="https://example.com" title="Click to visit the Example Website">Visit Example Website</a>
```

In this example, the `title` attribute adds extra information, which will be read aloud by screen readers.

- **Skip Navigation Links**: It's often helpful to include a "skip to content" link at the top of a page for users who navigate with keyboards, enabling them to skip past repetitive navigation menus.

```
<a href="#maincontent">Skip to Content</a>
```

3. Use `target="_blank"` Wisely

The `target="_blank"` attribute opens links in a new browser tab or window. While this behavior is often useful for external links, overusing it can cause frustration for users, especially those with many tabs open.

- **Use Sparingly**: Use `target="_blank"` primarily for external links or when you want users to remain on the original page while viewing the linked content.

```
<a href="https://externalwebsite.com" target="_blank">Visit External Website</a>
```

- **Security Considerations**: When using `target="_blank"`, it's essential to prevent potential security risks (such as phishing) by including `rel="noopener noreferrer"`. This prevents the newly opened tab from accessing the original page's `window` object.

```
<a href="https://externalwebsite.com" target="_blank" rel="noopener noreferrer">Visit External Website</a>
```

4. Test Links Regularly

Regular testing of your links is crucial to ensure they are functional and direct users to the correct destination. Broken or outdated links create a poor user experience and can harm the credibility of your website.

- **Check After Updates**: Whenever you update a page, check that all links, especially internal ones, still work and point to the correct resources.
- **Use Link Checkers**: Automated tools like **W3C Link Checker** or browser extensions can help identify broken links on your website.

Best Practices for Accessibility in HTML

Accessibility is about making web content usable for people with various disabilities. Here are some important HTML accessibility best practices:

---

1. Semantic HTML

Using semantic HTML tags improves both accessibility and SEO. Semantic tags describe the meaning of the content they contain, which helps screen readers and search engines understand the structure and purpose of your content.

- **Use Semantic Tags**: Instead of using generic `<div>` or `<span>` tags, use semantic HTML tags like `<header>`, `<footer>`, `<nav>`, and `<article>`.

  Example:

```
<header>
  <h1>Website Title</h1>
  <nav>
    <ul>
      <li><a href="#home">Home</a></li>
      <li><a href="#about">About</a></li>
    </ul>
  </nav>
</header>
```

- **Improves Screen Reader Navigation**: Semantic HTML helps screen readers map out the page structure, making it easier for visually impaired users to navigate.

---

2. Alt Text for Images

The `alt` attribute provides descriptive text for images, making them accessible to users who are visually impaired or using screen readers.

- **Always Provide Alt Text**: Use the `alt` attribute with all images to describe their content or function.

  ```
  <img src="logo.jpg" alt="Company Logo">
  ```

- **Descriptive and Concise**: The `alt` text should be clear, concise, and descriptive, accurately describing the content of the image.
- **Empty Alt Text for Decorative Images**: If the image is purely decorative and doesn't add meaningful content, you can leave the `alt` attribute empty (`alt=""`), so screen readers will ignore it.

  ```
  <img src="decorative.jpg" alt="">
  ```

3. Labels for Forms

Ensure that all form inputs have corresponding `<label>` elements. This improves accessibility by allowing screen readers to associate the label with the correct form element.

- **Use the `for` Attribute**: The `for` attribute in the `<label>` tag should match the `id` of the input element.

  ```
  <label for="username">Username:</label>
  <input type="text" id="username" name="username">
  ```

- **Invisible Labels**: If you need to hide labels for design reasons, use CSS to hide the label visually while keeping it accessible to screen readers.

4. Heading Structure

Headings provide structure to your page and help screen readers navigate the content. Always use headings in a logical, hierarchical order (from `<h1>` to `<h6>`) to organize content.

- **Use Only One `<h1>` per Page**: The `<h1>` tag is usually reserved for the main title or header of the page, indicating its primary content.
- **Subheadings**: Use `<h2>` to `<h6>` tags to structure sections and subsections logically.

5. Use of ARIA (Accessible Rich Internet Applications)

ARIA attributes help improve the accessibility of dynamic content and advanced user interface elements that are not natively accessible.

- **Example of ARIA Label**:

```
<button aria-label="Close">X</button>
```

The `aria-label` attribute provides a text description of the button's purpose, which is read by screen readers.

6. Accessible Navigation

Navigation links should be easy to use for all users. This means using clear, descriptive link text and ensuring the links are keyboard-navigable.

- **Logical Tab Order**: Ensure that users can navigate through your links and form elements in a logical order using the Tab key.
- **Keyboard Shortcuts**: Implement keyboard shortcuts where possible, allowing users to quickly navigate your site using the keyboard.

7. Responsive Design

Ensure that your HTML documents are mobile-friendly by using the `meta` viewport tag. This tag makes the page more accessible on devices with smaller screens, like smartphones and tablets.

- **Example of the Viewport Tag**:

```
<meta name="viewport" content="width=device-width, initial-scale=1.0">
```

- **Responsive Design**: Design your page to adapt to different screen sizes, ensuring users have a good experience regardless of the device they're using.

In conclusion, HTML is the backbone of any web page or web application, providing the structure needed to display content. Understanding how to use HTML tags, attributes, and elements properly helps you create well-structured, accessible, and user-friendly web pages. Best practices, like using semantic tags and providing alternative text for images, ensure your content is accessible to a wider audience.

50 multiple-choice questions (MCQs)

Introduction to HTML

1. **What does HTML stand for?**
   - o A) Hyper Transfer Markup Language
   - o B) HyperText Markup Language
   - o C) HyperLink Markup Language
   - o D) HyperLink Text Language
   - o **Answer**: B) HyperText Markup Language
2. **Which HTML tag is used to define a paragraph?**
   - o A) `<heading>`
   - o B) `<p>`
   - o C) `<para>`
   - o D) `<text>`
   - o **Answer**: B) `<p>`
3. **Which version of HTML is the latest?**
   - o A) HTML4
   - o B) XHTML
   - o C) HTML5
   - o D) HTML6
   - o **Answer**: C) HTML5
4. **Which of the following is the correct HTML for a link?**
   - o A) `<link href="url.com">`
   - o B) `<a href="url.com">`
   - o C) `<anchor href="url.com">`
   - o D) `<a src="url.com">`
   - o **Answer**: B) `<a href="url.com">`
5. **Which HTML tag is used to define an image?**
   - o A) `<picture>`
   - o B) `<img>`
   - o C) `<image>`
   - o D) `<src>`
   - o **Answer**: B) `<img>`

Basic Structure of an HTML Document

6. **Which tag is used to define the beginning of an HTML document?**
   - o A) `<html>`
   - o B) `<document>`
   - o C) `<head>`
   - o D) `<body>`
   - o **Answer**: A) `<html>`
7. **What tag is used to define the document metadata in HTML?**
   - o A) `<head>`
   - o B) `<title>`
   - o C) `<body>`

- D) `<footer>`
- **Answer:** A) `<head>`

8. **What is the purpose of the `<!DOCTYPE html>` declaration?**
    - A) It declares the HTML version being used.
    - B) It declares the type of the document.
    - C) It sets the content type for the HTML document.
    - D) It adds links to external resources.
    - **Answer:** A) It declares the HTML version being used.

9. **Which tag is used to define the main content of an HTML document?**
    - A) `<body>`
    - B) `<section>`
    - C) `<header>`
    - D) `<article>`
    - **Answer:** A) `<body>`

10. **Where is the title of a webpage defined in the HTML document?**
    - A) Inside `<body>`
    - B) Inside `<footer>`
    - C) Inside `<head>`
    - D) Inside `<article>`
    - **Answer:** C) Inside `<head>`

Elements, Tags, and Attributes

11. **Which part of an HTML element provides extra information about it?**
    - A) Tag
    - B) Content
    - C) Attribute
    - D) Element
    - **Answer:** C) Attribute

12. **What is the correct way to define a hyperlink in HTML?**
    - A) `<a name="url">`
    - B) `<a url="url.com">`
    - C) `<a href="url.com">`
    - D) `<link href="url.com">`
    - **Answer:** C) `<a href="url.com">`

13. **Which HTML tag is used for adding an image to a webpage?**
    - A) `<image>`
    - B) `<img>`
    - C) `<picture>`
    - D) `<src>`
    - **Answer:** B) `<img>`

14. **What does the `alt` attribute in an image tag do?**
    - A) Specifies the image file format.
    - B) Provides alternative text for the image.
    - C) Defines the image size.
    - D) Specifies the image source.
    - **Answer:** B) Provides alternative text for the image.

15. **Which tag is used to define a table in HTML?**
    - o A) `<table>`
    - o B) `<tab>`
    - o C) `<list>`
    - o D) `<data>`
    - o **Answer:** A) `<table>`

Common HTML Tags: Headings, Paragraphs, Links, Images, Forms

16. **What tag is used to define the most important heading?**
    - o A) `<h2>`
    - o B) `<h3>`
    - o C) `<h1>`
    - o D) `<heading>`
    - o **Answer:** C) `<h1>`
17. **Which tag is used to create a form in HTML?**
    - o A) `<input>`
    - o B) `<form>`
    - o C) `<button>`
    - o D) `<label>`
    - o **Answer:** B) `<form>`
18. **Which attribute is used to specify the URL for a link?**
    - o A) `src`
    - o B) `url`
    - o C) `href`
    - o D) `link`
    - o **Answer:** C) `href`
19. **How do you create a checkbox in a form?**
    - o A) `<input type="text">`
    - o B) `<input type="button">`
    - o C) `<input type="checkbox">`
    - o D) `<checkbox>`
    - o **Answer:** C) `<input type="checkbox">`
20. **Which HTML element is used for a paragraph of text?**
    - o A) `<text>`
    - o B) `<p>`
    - o C) `<para>`
    - o D) `<span>`
    - o **Answer:** B) `<p>`

Structuring Web Pages with Lists, Tables, and Forms

21. **Which tag is used to define an unordered list in HTML?**
    - o A) `<ul>`
    - o B) `<ol>`
    - o C) `<list>`
    - o D) `<li>`

o **Answer:** A) `<ul>`

22. **What tag is used to define a table row in HTML?**
    o A) `<tr>`
    o B) `<td>`
    o C) `<th>`
    o D) `<row>`
    o **Answer:** A) `<tr>`

23. **Which HTML tag defines a list item?**
    o A) `<li>`
    o B) `<list>`
    o C) `<item>`
    o D) `<ul>`
    o **Answer:** A) `<li>`

24. **Which of the following is the correct way to define a form field for entering text?**
    o A) `<forminput type="text">`
    o B) `<input type="text">`
    o C) `<input type="textbox">`
    o D) `<textfield type="text">`
    o **Answer:** B) `<input type="text">`

25. **How do you group form controls together in HTML?**
    o A) `<group>`
    o B) `<fieldset>`
    o C) `<div>`
    o D) `<section>`
    o **Answer:** B) `<fieldset>`

Creating Links and Navigating Between Pages

26. **How do you create a link to another page within the same website?**
    o A) `<a href="otherpage.html">`
    o B) `<link href="otherpage.html">`
    o C) `<goto link="otherpage.html">`
    o D) `<navigate href="otherpage.html">`
    o **Answer:** A) `<a href="otherpage.html">`

27. **What is the purpose of the `target="_blank"` attribute in a link?**
    o A) It opens the link in the current tab.
    o B) It opens the link in a new tab or window.
    o C) It opens the link in a modal window.
    o D) It disables the link.
    o **Answer:** B) It opens the link in a new tab or window.

28. **How do you create an anchor link that navigates to a specific section of the page?**
    o A) `<a href="#section1">Go to Section 1</a>`
    o B) `<a href="section1.html">Go to Section 1</a>`
    o C) `<a link="#section1">Go to Section 1</a>`
    o D) `<a target="#section1">Go to Section 1</a>`
    o **Answer:** A) `<a href="#section1">Go to Section 1</a>`

29. **Which of the following is the correct HTML for opening a link in a new window?**
     - A) `<a href="http://example.com" target="_blank">Visit Example</a>`
     - B) `<a href="http://example.com" open="new">Visit Example</a>`
     - C) `<link href="http://example.com" target="_new">Visit Example</a>`
     - D) `<a href="http://example.com" open="window">Visit Example</a>`
     - **Answer**: A) `<a href="http://example.com" target="_blank">Visit Example</a>`

30. **What is the `href` attribute used for in HTML links?**
     - A) It specifies the type of the link.
     - B) It specifies the destination URL of the link.
     - C) It opens the link in a new tab.
     - D) It defines the link's display text.
     - **Answer**: B) It specifies the destination URL of the link.

Best Practices and Accessibility in HTML

31. **Which of the following is an accessibility best practice for HTML links?**
     - A) Use generic link text like "Click here."
     - B) Use descriptive link text, like "Read more about accessibility."
     - C) Open all links in new windows.
     - D) Use JavaScript links only.
     - **Answer**: B) Use descriptive link text, like "Read more about accessibility."

32. **Why is semantic HTML important for accessibility?**
     - A) It makes the page look nicer.
     - B) It helps search engines understand the content.
     - C) It ensures the content is usable by screen readers.
     - D) It reduces the page size.
     - **Answer**: C) It ensures the content is usable by screen readers.

33. **What should you include for images to make them accessible to screen readers?**
     - A) Use empty `alt` attributes.
     - B) Use descriptive text in the `alt` attribute.
     - C) Use `alt=""` for decorative images.
     - D) Both B and C.
     - **Answer**: D) Both B and C.

34. **How can you ensure that a form is accessible?**
     - A) Use labels for form fields.
     - B) Use placeholder text instead of labels.
     - C) Use form controls without labels.
     - D) Avoid using forms.
     - **Answer**: A) Use labels for form fields.

35. **What is the purpose of the `<label>` tag in HTML?**
     - A) To create a clickable label for form elements.
     - B) To format text.
     - C) To define the input type.
     - D) To group form elements.

- o **Answer**: A) To create a clickable label for form elements.

36. What is a good practice for headings in HTML?
- o A) Use only `<h1>` tags for all headings.
- o B) Use headings in a hierarchical order (`<h1>` to `<h6>`).
- o C) Use headings for styling purposes.
- o D) Use headings to organize paragraphs.
- o **Answer**: B) Use headings in a hierarchical order (`<h1>` to `<h6>`).

37. Which HTML element should be used for page navigation?
- o A) `<footer>`
- o B) `<header>`
- o C) `<nav>`
- o D) `<section>`
- o **Answer**: C) `<nav>`

38. What does the `aria-label` attribute do?
- o A) Provides an accessible name for an element.
- o B) Labels form inputs.
- o C) Adds a title to the page.
- o D) Changes the font size of the label.
- o **Answer**: A) Provides an accessible name for an element.

39. How can you make a page responsive for mobile devices?
- o A) Use fixed width for layout.
- o B) Use the `<meta>` viewport tag.
- o C) Disable scaling.
- o D) Use tables for layout.
- o **Answer**: B) Use the `<meta>` viewport tag.

40. What is the primary role of the `<footer>` tag in HTML?
- o A) To define the header section of a page.
- o B) To define a navigation menu.
- o C) To define the content at the bottom of the page.
- o D) To group article content.
- o **Answer**: C) To define the content at the bottom of the page.

General HTML Questions

41. What is the purpose of the `alt` attribute in the `<img>` tag?
- o A) To define the image size.
- o B) To provide alternative text for the image.
- o C) To set the image source.
- o D) To set the image format.
- o **Answer**: B) To provide alternative text for the image.

42. Which HTML tag is used to create a button?
- o A) `<btn>`
- o B) `<button>`
- o C) `<input type="button">`
- o D) Both B and C

- o **Answer**: D) Both B and C

43. How do you make a list ordered in HTML?

- o A) Use the `<ol>` tag.
- o B) Use the `<ul>` tag.
- o C) Use the `<list>` tag.
- o D) Use the `<li>` tag.
- o **Answer**: A) Use the `<ol>` tag.

44. Which tag is used to group together inline elements in HTML?

- o A) `<span>`
- o B) `<div>`
- o C) `<section>`
- o D) `<group>`
- o **Answer**: A) `<span>`

45. How can you make a webpage accessible for screen readers?

- o A) Use semantic HTML tags.
- o B) Provide text alternatives for images.
- o C) Use clear, descriptive headings.
- o D) All of the above.
- o **Answer**: D) All of the above.

46. Which tag is used to specify the character encoding in an HTML document?

- o A) `<meta>`
- o B) `<charset>`
- o C) `<head>`
- o D) `<encoding>`
- o **Answer**: A) `<meta>`

47. What does the `placeholder` attribute do in HTML forms?

- o A) It adds a default value to the input field.
- o B) It creates a label for the input field.
- o C) It shows a short description inside the input field when empty.
- o D) It disables the input field.
- o **Answer**: C) It shows a short description inside the input field when empty.

48. How do you create a drop-down list in HTML?

- o A) `<input type="select">`
- o B) `<select>`
- o C) `<option>`
- o D) `<dropdown>`
- o **Answer**: B) `<select>`

49. What is the role of the `meta` tag in HTML?

- o A) It defines metadata about the HTML document.
- o B) It formats text.
- o C) It links external resources.
- o D) It defines the header.
- o **Answer**: A) It defines metadata about the HTML document.

50. Which tag is used to define an ordered list?

- o A) `<ul>`
- o B) `<ol>`
- o C) `<list>`

- o D) `<li>`
- o **Answer**: B) `<ol>`

50 questions and answers

Introduction to HTML

1. **What does HTML stand for?**
   - o **Answer:** HTML stands for HyperText Markup Language.
2. **What is the primary role of HTML in web development?**
   - o **Answer:** HTML provides the structure for web pages by defining content using a system of elements and tags.
3. **Which of the following is a correct HTML tag to create a hyperlink?**
   - o **Answer:** `<a href="url">Link Text</a>`
4. **Which HTML tag is used to define a paragraph?**
   - o **Answer:** `<p>`
5. **In which tag is the title of the webpage placed?**
   - o **Answer:** The title is placed inside the `<title>` tag, which is within the `<head>` section.

Basic Structure of an HTML Document

6. **What tag is used to define the root of an HTML document?**
   - o **Answer:** `<html>`
7. **What is the purpose of the `<!DOCTYPE html>` declaration?**
   - o **Answer:** It defines the document type and version of HTML being used (HTML5).
8. **Where do you place the metadata of an HTML document?**
   - o **Answer:** Inside the `<head>` tag.
9. **What is the function of the `<body>` tag?**
   - o **Answer:** The `<body>` tag contains the visible content of the web page that users can see and interact with.
10. **Which tag is used to define a section in the document for storing metadata like character set and viewport information?**

- • **Answer:** `<head>`

Elements, Tags, and Attributes

11. **What is an HTML element?**

- • **Answer:** An HTML element consists of an opening tag, content, and a closing tag.

12. **Which part of an HTML element specifies extra information about the element?**

- **Answer:** The attribute specifies extra information about an element.

13. **Which HTML tag is used to define an image?**

- **Answer:** `<img>`

14. **Which attribute is used to specify the source of an image?**

- **Answer:** `src`

15. **What does the `alt` attribute in the `<img>` tag do?**

- **Answer:** The `alt` attribute provides alternative text for an image, important for accessibility and when images can't be displayed.

Common HTML Tags: Headings, Paragraphs, Links, Images, Forms

16. **How many levels of headings does HTML provide?**

- **Answer:** HTML provides six levels of headings, from `<h1>` to `<h6>`, with `<h1>` being the highest level.

17. **What tag is used to define a hyperlink in HTML?**

- **Answer:** `<a>`

18. **Which attribute of the `<a>` tag is used to specify the destination URL?**

- **Answer:** The `href` attribute.

19. **Which tag is used to define an ordered list?**

- **Answer:** `<ol>`

20. **How do you specify a text input field in a form?**

- **Answer:** `<input type="text">`

Structuring Web Pages with Lists, Tables, and Forms

21. **Which tag is used to define a table in HTML?**

- **Answer:** `<table>`

22. **What tag is used to create a table row?**

- **Answer:** `<tr>`

23. **Which tag is used to define a cell in a table?**

- **Answer:** `<td>`

24. **How do you create a drop-down list in HTML?**

- **Answer:** `<select>` along with `<option>` tags.

25. **What tag is used to define a form in HTML?**

- **Answer:** `<form>`

26. **Which tag is used to define a list item in both unordered and ordered lists?**

- **Answer:** `<li>`

27. **Which HTML tag is used for form buttons?**

- **Answer:** `<button>`

28. **What tag is used to define a header for a table in HTML?**

- **Answer:** `<th>`

29. **What tag is used to group together multiple form elements?**

- **Answer:** `<fieldset>`

30. **What attribute is used to specify the method for sending form data?**

- **Answer:** The `method` attribute (e.g., `method="post"` or `method="get"`).

Creating Links and Navigating Between Pages

31. **How do you link to an external website in HTML?**

- **Answer:** Use the `<a>` tag with the `href` attribute, e.g., `<a href="https://example.com">Visit Example</a>`.

32. **What attribute is used to specify that a link should open in a new window or tab?**

- **Answer:** The `target="_blank"` attribute.

33. **How can you create an anchor link that navigates to a section within the same page?**

- **Answer:** Use an anchor link with the `href` attribute pointing to the `id` of the section, e.g., `<a href="#section1">Go to Section 1</a>`.

34. **What is the purpose of the `title` attribute in an anchor tag?**

- **Answer:** The `title` attribute provides additional information when a user hovers over the link.

35. **Which tag is used to specify a clickable image in HTML?**

- **Answer:** The `<a>` tag combined with an `<img>` tag, e.g., `<a href="page.html"><img src="image.jpg" alt="Description"></a>`.

Best Practices and Accessibility in HTML

36. **What is semantic HTML?**

- **Answer:** Semantic HTML uses meaningful and descriptive tags to structure content in a way that is both machine-readable and accessible.

37. **Why is it important to use `alt` attributes for images?**

- **Answer:** `alt` attributes provide a description for users who are visually impaired and use screen readers, as well as when the image cannot be displayed.

38. **How can you ensure accessibility when creating forms?**

- **Answer:** By using `<label>` elements for form inputs to associate the label text with the corresponding input field.

39. **Why should you avoid using generic link text like "Click here"?**

- **Answer:** Generic link text does not provide context to users and can negatively affect accessibility, making it harder for screen readers to convey useful information.

40. **What is the role of the `aria-label` attribute in HTML?**

- **Answer:** The `aria-label` attribute is used to provide an accessible name for elements that may not have a visible label, helping screen readers understand the content.

41. **What tag is used to define the header section of an HTML document?**

- **Answer:** `<header>`

42. **How can you make your HTML page mobile-friendly?**

- **Answer:** By including the `<meta>` tag for the viewport in the `<head>` section, e.g., `<meta name="viewport" content="width=device-width, initial-scale=1.0">`.

43. **What is the purpose of the `<footer>` tag in HTML?**

- **Answer:** The `<footer>` tag defines the footer section of a webpage, typically containing copyright information, contact details, or links to privacy policies.

44. **How can you improve the readability of your HTML code?**

- **Answer:** By using proper indentation, comments, and clear naming conventions for elements.

45. **What does the `aria-live` attribute do?**

- **Answer:** The `aria-live` attribute notifies assistive technologies when content changes dynamically, improving accessibility for users with disabilities.

Other HTML Practices

46. **What is the purpose of using the `<meta charset="UTF-8">` tag in HTML?**

- **Answer:** It specifies the character encoding for the document, ensuring the proper display of characters, including non-English characters.

47. **What is the best way to include a JavaScript file in an HTML document?**

- **Answer:** By using the `<script>` tag, e.g., `<script src="script.js"></script>`, typically placed just before the closing `</body>` tag.

48. **How can you create a table with a header and two rows of data?**

- **Answer:** Use the `<table>`, `<tr>`, `<th>`, and `<td>` tags, e.g.:

```
<table>
```

```
<tr>
  <th>Header 1</th>
  <th>Header 2</th>
</tr>
<tr>
  <td>Data 1</td>
  <td>Data 2</td>
</tr>
</table>
```

49. **What does the `required` attribute do in HTML form elements?**

- **Answer:** It specifies that a form field must be filled out before submitting the form.

50. **What is the function of the `<style>` tag in an HTML document?**

- **Answer:** The `<style>` tag is used to define internal CSS rules that style the content of the HTML document.

CHAPTER 2: INTRODUCTION TO XHTML (EXTENSIBLE HYPERTEXT MARKUP LANGUAGE)

What is XHTML and How is it Different from HTML?

XHTML (Extensible Hypertext Markup Language) is an updated version of HTML that incorporates the stricter syntax rules of XML (Extensible Markup Language). It was developed by the W3C (World Wide Web Consortium) to provide better document structure, error handling, and improve compatibility across different devices, browsers, and web technologies.

XHTML is essentially HTML that is reformulated to comply with the syntax rules and structure of XML. This means that, while it maintains backward compatibility with HTML, it adheres to stricter coding practices, allowing web documents to be processed by XML parsers as well as HTML parsers. In simple terms, XHTML is HTML with a more rigorous structure that makes it suitable for stricter validation.

Key Differences Between XHTML and HTML:

1. Strict Syntax:

- **XHTML** enforces strict syntax rules derived from XML. This includes:
    - **Closing Tags:** Every element in XHTML must be properly closed, even for self-closing or void elements (such as `<img>`, `<br>`, or `<hr>`).
        - Example:
            - In HTML, `<img src="image.jpg">` is valid, but in XHTML, it must be `<img src="image.jpg" />`.
    - **Lowercase Elements and Attributes:** All elements and attributes in XHTML must be written in lowercase. HTML is case-insensitive, so tags like `<TITLE>` and `<title>` would be treated the same, but XHTML requires `<title>` to be lowercase.
        - Example: `<div>` is correct in XHTML, but `<DIV>` would be invalid.
    - **Well-formed Documents:** XHTML requires the document structure to be perfect. This means that all tags must be correctly nested, and there can be no unclosed or improperly nested tags.
        - Example:
            - HTML may allow: `<div><p>Text</div></p>` (which browsers will auto-correct).
            - In XHTML, this would be incorrect, and the tags must be properly nested like: `<div><p>Text</p></div>`.
- **HTML**, on the other hand, is more lenient. If a tag is missing or improperly nested, browsers usually correct or ignore the issue, allowing the page to render, albeit not necessarily according to standards.

2. Well-formed Documents:

- **XHTML** documents must be well-formed XML documents. In XML, all tags must be closed, and elements must be properly nested. If any element is left unclosed or improperly nested, it will cause the document to be considered invalid.
    - o Example:
        - ▪ In HTML, a paragraph tag like `<p>This is a paragraph` (without a closing `</p>`) may still render in the browser.
        - ▪ In XHTML, this would result in an error, and the page would not be displayed unless the closing `</p>` tag is added.
- **HTML** offers more leniency, meaning it can handle errors like unclosed tags and continue rendering the page.

3. Document Declaration:

- **XHTML** requires a specific `DOCTYPE` declaration to ensure it is parsed as an XML document. The declaration specifies the XHTML version being used and provides the rules that the document must follow.
    - o Example:

        ```
        <!DOCTYPE html PUBLIC "-//W3C//DTD XHTML 1.0 Strict//EN"
        "http://www.w3.org/TR/xhtml1/DTD/xhtml1-strict.dtd">
        ```

- **HTML**, specifically HTML5, uses a simpler `DOCTYPE` declaration:
    - o Example:

        ```
        <!DOCTYPE html>
        ```

    - o The difference in declaration highlights the fact that HTML5 is more flexible, whereas XHTML requires a more specific, rigid structure for correct parsing and validation.

4. Error Handling:

- **XHTML** follows strict error handling rules. If there is any mistake or violation of syntax, such as unclosed tags or improperly nested elements, the document will fail to render in browsers that support XML.
    - o If an XHTML document is invalid, XML parsers (such as the ones used by web browsers) will refuse to render it, potentially displaying an error message.
- **HTML**, in contrast, is more forgiving with errors. Web browsers that render HTML will often correct minor issues like missing closing tags or improperly nested elements, allowing the page to display even if there are mistakes in the code.

Summary of Differences Between XHTML and HTML:

Aspect	HTML	XHTML
Syntax	More lenient with syntax (e.g., missing tags or improper nesting are allowed)	Strict syntax, requiring well-formed XML documents
Tags and Attributes Case	Case-insensitive for tags and attributes	All tags and attributes must be in lowercase
Tag Closure	Tags may be left unclosed, browser auto-corrects	All tags must be properly closed, including self-closing tags (e.g., `<img />`)
Error Handling	Browsers tolerate errors and continue rendering	Browsers refuse to render invalid XHTML documents
DOCTYPE Declaration	Simple `<!DOCTYPE html>` declaration for HTML5	Specific `DOCTYPE` declaration with an XML schema (e.g., XHTML 1.0 Strict)
Document Compatibility	Works in both XML and HTML parsers	Can be processed by both XML and HTML parsers

Why Was XHTML Created?

XHTML was created to address some of the limitations of HTML and ensure that web documents could be parsed by both HTML and XML parsers. The major goals of XHTML were:

1. **Cleaner Code**: Encouraging well-formed, structured, and more predictable web pages.
2. **Better Error Handling**: XHTML's strictness was intended to make it easier to detect and correct errors during development, improving the reliability of web documents.
3. **Cross-platform Compatibility**: XHTML aimed to provide better compatibility across a variety of devices and platforms, as XML parsers could be used to process the document's content in addition to traditional HTML parsers.
4. **Web Standards Compliance**: XHTML followed stricter web standards, ensuring that web content would be more accessible, consistent, and reliable.

However, as web development has evolved, **HTML5** has become the preferred choice for creating modern web pages. HTML5 provides more flexibility and removes some of the strict constraints that XHTML imposed, while still adhering to many of the best practices introduced by XHTML, such as cleaner and well-structured code.

Strict Syntax and Well-formed Documents

XHTML (Extensible Hypertext Markup Language) is based on XML (Extensible Markup Language) and requires web documents to follow strict syntax rules. This ensures that all HTML elements are structured in a well-formed manner, making them more predictable and easier to parse. Below, we explore the critical principles of **strict syntax** and **well-formed documents** in XHTML.

Key Principles of Strict Syntax and Well-formed Documents in XHTML:

1. Proper Tag Closure:

- **Requirement:** Every tag in XHTML must have an opening tag and a corresponding closing tag. This rule applies to all HTML elements, including void elements (tags that do not have content).
- **Explanation:** XHTML is based on XML, which requires every tag to be properly opened and closed. This is in contrast to HTML, which is more forgiving and allows certain tags (like `<p>`) to be automatically closed by the browser if missing.
- **Examples:**
  - **Correct:**

    ```
    <p>This is a paragraph.</p>
    ```

  - **Correct for self-closing tags:**

    ```
    <img src="image.jpg" alt="Image" />
    ```

    In XHTML, even self-closing tags like `<img>` must end with a slash (/) to signify that they are self-contained.

  - **Incorrect in XHTML (unclosed tags):**

    ```
    <p>This is a paragraph.
    ```

    In XHTML, this would result in an error because the `<p>` tag has not been closed.

---

2. Lowercase Tags and Attributes:

- **Requirement:** XHTML requires all tags and attributes to be written in lowercase, unlike HTML where uppercase tags were allowed.
- **Explanation:** Since XHTML is based on XML, which is case-sensitive, it is essential to use lowercase for all element names and attribute names. This ensures consistency and compatibility with XML parsers.

- **Examples:**
  - ○ **Correct:**

    ```
    <a href="https://example.com">Link</a>
    ```

  - ○ **Incorrect (uppercase tags and attributes):**

    ```
    <A HREF="https://example.com">Link</A>
    ```

    In XHTML, the `<A>` and `HREF` tags must be lowercase: `<a href="...">`.

---

3. Proper Nesting:

- **Requirement:** In XHTML, elements must be properly nested. This means that no element can be improperly closed, and the hierarchy must be respected.
- **Explanation:** XHTML documents must have a consistent structure. Elements must be properly opened and closed, and no tags can be placed inside other tags incorrectly. This ensures that the document is "well-formed" according to XML standards.
- **Examples:**
  - ○ **Correct:**

    ```
    <div><p>Hello</p></div>
    ```

  - ○ **Incorrect (improperly nested tags):**

    ```
    <div><p>Hello</div></p>
    ```

    In XHTML, the tags must be properly nested, so `<p>` must be closed before `<div>` is closed.

---

4. No Implicit Closing of Tags:

- **Requirement:** In XHTML, there is no automatic closing of tags. Every tag, including block-level tags like `<p>`, must be explicitly closed. This contrasts with HTML, where browsers often auto-correct missing closing tags (for instance, automatically closing `<p>` tags when needed).
- **Explanation:** XHTML strictly requires that every tag be explicitly opened and closed, preventing any ambiguity in document structure. This avoids rendering issues and ensures the document is predictable across different browsers and parsers.
- **Example:**
  - ○ **Correct in XHTML:**

    ```
    <p>This is a paragraph.</p>
    ```

- Incorrect in XHTML:

```
<p>This is a paragraph.
```

In HTML, this would work fine in most browsers (due to auto-closing behavior), but in XHTML, it will not render correctly unless the closing `</p>` tag is included.

---

5. Attribute Quotation:

- **Requirement:** In XHTML, all attribute values must be enclosed in quotation marks, regardless of whether the value contains spaces or not.
- **Explanation:** XHTML follows the XML standard, which requires that attributes always be quoted. This helps to avoid ambiguity in parsing and ensures consistency in the document structure. In HTML, quoting attributes was optional in certain cases, but XHTML mandates this rule to ensure that all documents are well-formed.
- **Examples:**
    - **Correct:**

    ```
    <img src="image.jpg" alt="Description of image" />
    ```

    - **Incorrect (missing quotations):**

    ```
    <img src=image.jpg alt=Description />
    ```

    In XHTML, the attribute values `src=image.jpg` and `alt=Description` must be enclosed in quotes (`src="image.jpg"` and `alt="Description"`), or the document will be considered invalid.

Summary of Strict Syntax and Well-formed Documents in XHTML:

Principle	Explanation	Example (Correct)	Example (Incorrect)
Proper Tag Closure	Every tag must have both opening and closing tags (self-closing tags must end with a slash).	`<p>This is a paragraph.</p>`	`<p>This is a paragraph.`
Lowercase Tags and Attributes	Tags and attributes must be written in lowercase to adhere to XML standards.	`<a href="example.com">Link</a>`	`<A HREF="example.com">Link</A>`
Proper Nesting	Elements must be properly nested, with no overlapping or misplaced tags.	`<div><p>Hello</p></div>`	`<div><p>Hello</div></p>`
No Implicit Closing of Tags	Tags must always be explicitly closed, and browsers cannot automatically fix missing or mismatched tags.	`<p>This is a paragraph.</p>`	`<p>This is a paragraph.`
Attribute Quotation	All attribute values must be enclosed in quotation marks.	`<img src="image.jpg" alt="Image" />`	`<img src=image.jpg alt=Image />`

By following these strict syntax rules, XHTML ensures that web documents are well-structured, consistent, and compliant with XML standards, which helps improve compatibility with a wider range of browsers and parsers.

Creating XHTML Pages: Syntax Rules and Examples

Creating an XHTML page requires adherence to specific syntax rules to ensure the document is well-formed and complies with XHTML standards. XHTML is a stricter version of HTML, based on XML (Extensible Markup Language), and therefore follows XML rules. Below is a detailed explanation of the syntax rules when creating an XHTML document, along with an example.

Example of a Simple XHTML Document:

```
<!DOCTYPE html PUBLIC "-//W3C//DTD XHTML 1.0 Strict//EN"
"http://www.w3.org/TR/xhtml1/DTD/xhtml1-strict.dtd">
<html xmlns="http://www.w3.org/1999/xhtml">
  <head>
    <meta charset="UTF-8" />
    <title>My XHTML Page</title>
  </head>
  <body>
    <h1>Welcome to My XHTML Page</h1>
    <p>This is a simple XHTML document.</p>
    <img src="image.jpg" alt="An image" />
  </body>
</html>
```

Key Syntax Rules in XHTML:

1. DOCTYPE Declaration:

- **Rule:** The `<!DOCTYPE>` declaration defines the document type and specifies the version of XHTML being used.
- **Explanation:** The `<!DOCTYPE>` declaration tells the browser which version of XHTML it should expect. It also triggers the browser's rendering engine to display the page in standards mode. The declaration for XHTML 1.0 Strict is shown in the example.
- **Example:**

  ```
  <!DOCTYPE html PUBLIC "-//W3C//DTD XHTML 1.0 Strict//EN"
  "http://www.w3.org/TR/xhtml1/DTD/xhtml1-strict.dtd">
  ```

  - This declaration specifies that the document adheres to **XHTML 1.0 Strict** and should conform to the strict rules defined by the W3C.

2. HTML Namespace (xmlns):

- **Rule:** The `xmlns` attribute in the `<html>` tag defines the XML namespace for XHTML.

- **Explanation:** XHTML documents need to declare the XML namespace (`xmlns="http://www.w3.org/1999/xhtml"`) to comply with XML syntax rules. The XML namespace helps the browser differentiate XHTML elements from other XML-based documents.
- **Example:**

```
<html xmlns="http://www.w3.org/1999/xhtml">
```

  - This ensures that the document uses XHTML-specific tags and features. Without this declaration, the document would not be treated as XHTML by XML parsers.

---

3. Proper Tag Closure:

- **Rule:** Every tag must be properly closed, including self-closing tags like `<img>`.
- **Explanation:** In XHTML, all elements, including void elements (those that don't have a closing tag), must be self-closed by including a slash (`/`) before the closing angle bracket (`>`). This is a requirement of XML and ensures that the document is well-formed.
- **Examples:**
  - **Correct:**

```
<img src="image.jpg" alt="An image" />
```

    In XHTML, the `<img>` tag must be self-closed using the `/>` syntax, which is mandatory in XML.

  - **Incorrect in XHTML (unclosed tags):**

```
<img src="image.jpg" alt="An image">
```

    The `<img>` tag without the slash is incorrect in XHTML, as it violates the strict closing rule.

---

4. Case Sensitivity:

- **Rule:** Tags and attributes must be written in lowercase letters.
- **Explanation:** XHTML is case-sensitive (as it is based on XML), so it requires all HTML tags and attributes to be in lowercase. This is one of the key differences from HTML, which was case-insensitive.
- **Examples:**
  - **Correct:**

```
<html>
<head>
<body>
<h1>Welcome to My XHTML Page</h1>
```

    o **Incorrect:**

```
<HTML>
<HEAD>
<BODY>
<H1>Welcome to My XHTML Page</H1>
```

In XHTML, `<HTML>`, `<HEAD>`, `<BODY>`, and `<H1>` are considered incorrect because they use uppercase letters. All tags and attributes must be lowercase.

Other Important Syntax Rules:

5. Attribute Quotation:

- **Rule:** All attribute values must be enclosed in quotation marks.
- **Explanation:** In XHTML, all attribute values must be enclosed in double (" ") or single (' ') quotes, even if the attribute value does not contain spaces. This is required for all attributes to ensure proper parsing by XML parsers.
- **Example:**

```
<a href="https://www.example.com">Click Here</a>
```

- **Incorrect:**

```
<a href=https://www.example.com>Click Here</a>
```

In XHTML, the `href` attribute must be enclosed in quotation marks.

---

6. Empty Elements Must Be Self-closed:

- **Rule:** Tags for elements that do not have content (empty elements) must be self-closed.
- **Explanation:** In XHTML, void elements such as `<img>`, `<br>`, `<hr>`, and `<link>` must have a closing slash (/) within the opening tag.
- **Examples:**
  - **Correct:**

```
<br />
<hr />
```

  - **Incorrect:**

```
<br>
<hr>
```

In XHTML, these elements must include the self-closing slash (/), or they will cause errors when processed by XML parsers.

Full Example of a Well-formed XHTML Document:

```
<!DOCTYPE html PUBLIC "-//W3C//DTD XHTML 1.0 Strict//EN"
"http://www.w3.org/TR/xhtml1/DTD/xhtml1-strict.dtd">
<html xmlns="http://www.w3.org/1999/xhtml">
  <head>
    <meta charset="UTF-8" />
    <title>My XHTML Page</title>
  </head>
  <body>
    <h1>Welcome to My XHTML Page</h1>
    <p>This is a simple XHTML document.</p>
    <a href="https://www.example.com" target="_blank">Visit Example</a>
    <img src="image.jpg" alt="An image" />
    <br />
    <hr />
  </body>
</html>
```

Recap of Key Syntax Rules for Creating XHTML Pages:

1. **DOCTYPE Declaration:** Defines the document type and specifies the XHTML version.
2. **HTML Namespace:** Specifies the XML namespace to differentiate XHTML from other XML-based documents.
3. **Proper Tag Closure:** All tags must be properly closed, including self-closing tags.
4. **Case Sensitivity:** Tags and attributes must be written in lowercase.
5. **Attribute Quotation:** Attribute values must always be enclosed in quotation marks.
6. **Self-closing Void Elements:** Void elements must be properly self-closed using a slash (/).

XHTML and Web Standards

XHTML (Extensible HyperText Markup Language) was developed to address the limitations of HTML by making web pages more reliable, consistent, and accessible. XHTML enforces stricter coding standards and adheres to XML (Extensible Markup Language) rules, improving document structure, readability, and compatibility across different platforms.

Here's a detailed explanation of XHTML and its relationship to web standards, along with how it aligns with best practices for creating web content:

1. Cross-platform Compatibility

- **XHTML ensures consistent display across different platforms and devices:**
  - **Explanation:** One of XHTML's goals is to provide a more reliable and consistent way to display web pages across various devices, operating systems, and browsers. By adhering to stricter syntax rules, XHTML minimizes the risk of browser incompatibilities and ensures that web pages can be processed correctly by both web browsers and mobile devices, including those with limited capabilities.
  - **Impact on Mobile and Screen Readers:**
    - XHTML's structure benefits accessibility tools like **screen readers**, which are used by visually impaired users to interact with web content. Since XHTML documents are well-formed and predictable, they are easier for assistive technologies to parse and present.
    - **Mobile Devices:** As mobile browsing became more prominent, XHTML ensured that web pages could be rendered properly across different screen sizes and devices.

2. Cleaner Code

- **XHTML enforces a stricter structure, leading to more maintainable and readable code:**
  - **Explanation:** Unlike HTML, where browsers can often "guess" how to display content even with improperly closed tags or other syntax errors, XHTML enforces **strict syntax rules**. These rules require developers to:
    - Close all tags.
    - Write attributes in lowercase.
    - Properly nest elements.
    - Close void elements (e.g., `<img>`, `<br>`, `<hr>`) with a slash (/).
  - **Benefit:** By forcing developers to write cleaner and more structured code, XHTML makes web pages easier to maintain. Errors are more easily detected, and the document is less prone to unexpected behavior across different platforms.
  - **Cleaner Code Example:**
    - XHTML forces explicit closure of tags, such as:

      ```
      <img src="image.jpg" alt="Image description" />
      ```

    - In contrast, HTML might allow:

      ```
      <img src="image.jpg" alt="Image description">
      ```

      This can lead to issues with some browsers or document parsers, especially in complex documents.

3. Better Accessibility

- **XHTML contributes to better accessibility by ensuring content is well-structured and easier to process:**
  - **Explanation:** One of the main goals of XHTML is to improve the accessibility of web content for users with disabilities. Since XHTML enforces strict syntax rules and ensures proper nesting of elements, it helps assistive technologies like **screen readers** better interpret web content. Screen readers rely on predictable, well-formed documents to convert the content into speech or braille for visually impaired users.
  - **Key Accessibility Benefits of XHTML:**
    - **Proper Structure:** With XHTML, content is more logically structured, and headings, paragraphs, and links are clearly defined. This makes it easier for users to navigate a website using screen readers or other assistive tools.
    - **Consistent Code:** XHTML's strict rules, such as ensuring proper closure of all tags, help eliminate the ambiguity that might exist in improperly structured HTML documents.
    - **Semantic HTML:** XHTML encourages the use of appropriate tags for different types of content, such as `<article>`, `<header>`, `<footer>`, and `<nav>`. This supports better content parsing by assistive technologies.

4. Validation of XHTML Code

- **XHTML allows for easy validation through W3C XML validators:**
  - **Explanation:** One of the core features of XHTML is that it can be validated using **XML validators**, like those provided by the **W3C** (World Wide Web Consortium). Validation ensures that the document complies with XHTML standards, identifying errors in the markup that could prevent it from being rendered correctly by browsers.
  - **Benefits of Validation:**
    - **Error Detection:** Validation helps detect errors early in the development process, allowing developers to fix issues before they become problematic.
    - **Consistency:** Ensures that all XHTML documents conform to a standard structure, making web content more predictable across different platforms.
    - **Improved Performance:** A well-validated document is more likely to perform better, as it eliminates ambiguities and potential rendering problems.

    W3C XHTML Validator: The W3C provides a validation tool to check whether XHTML documents conform to the correct syntax and rules. Developers can upload or input their XHTML code to ensure it is well-formed and valid.

5. Transition to HTML5

- **XHTML was initially developed to improve upon HTML, but modern web development trends have shifted towards HTML5:**

- o **Explanation:** XHTML was a significant improvement over HTML, but modern web development trends have largely moved towards **HTML5** as the preferred standard for building web applications. HTML5 is more flexible, supports multimedia natively (audio, video, canvas), and combines the user-friendly nature of HTML with many of the structural benefits of XHTML. HTML5 allows for more natural syntax and is less strict in terms of the document's structure compared to XHTML.
- o **Comparison:**
  - **HTML5 vs XHTML**: HTML5 provides more freedom in terms of syntax (it is not case-sensitive, and closing tags are optional in some cases), but it still offers the semantic structure and accessibility benefits that were initially the goal of XHTML.
  - **Adoption of HTML5:** HTML5 has been widely adopted across the web, offering features like new semantic tags (`<article>`, `<section>`, `<header>`, `<footer>`) that make content more accessible and SEO-friendly.

6. When to Use XHTML

- **XHTML is still used in specific scenarios that require strict compliance with XML rules:**
  - o **Explanation:** While HTML5 is now the most commonly used standard for modern web applications, XHTML is still applicable in certain specialized situations. For example:
    - **XML-based Applications:** XHTML is appropriate for applications or environments that need a strict XML-based syntax (e.g., mobile applications, content management systems, or systems that require precise XML parsing).
    - **Compatibility with XML Parsers:** In situations where XML parsers are involved in processing web data (such as APIs, RSS feeds, or dynamic content generation), XHTML ensures better interoperability and reliability.

Validating XHTML Code

Validation is the process of ensuring that the code adheres to the syntax rules and standards of XHTML. Proper validation helps detect errors early in the development process and ensures that web documents are well-formed, accessible, and compatible across different browsers and devices. The W3C (World Wide Web Consortium) provides a validation service to check whether an XHTML document follows the proper structure and complies with XHTML standards.

Steps for Validating XHTML

1. Use W3C Validator

The **W3C Markup Validation Service** is an online tool that allows developers to check whether their XHTML documents are correctly formatted. This tool analyzes the document against XHTML specifications and points out any issues related to:

- Missing end tags.
- Incorrect tag nesting.
- Improper case usage.
- Missing DOCTYPE declaration.
- Other syntax issues that violate XHTML rules.

How to Use the W3C Validator:

- **Step 1:** Go to the <u>W3C Markup Validation Service</u>.
- **Step 2:** Input the URL of the page you want to validate or upload the XHTML file directly.
- **Step 3:** Click on "Check" to begin the validation process.
- **Step 4:** Review the results to identify any validation errors or warnings.

The W3C validator will provide a detailed list of issues along with explanations to help you fix them.

---

2. Fix Syntax Errors

Once the validator identifies issues in the XHTML code, the next step is to fix them. Common syntax errors in XHTML include:

- **Missing closing tags:** XHTML requires that all elements have corresponding closing tags (e.g., `<p></p>`, `<h1></h1>`), and void elements (like `<img>`, `<br>`) must be self-closed with a slash (`/>`).
- **Incorrect tag nesting:** In XHTML, elements must be properly nested, meaning one element cannot contain another element that isn't closed correctly.
    - **Correct:** `<div><p>Content</p></div>`
    - **Incorrect:** `<div><p>Content</div></p>`

When using the W3C validator, it will display the exact location of the error and suggest how to fix it.

Example:

If you forget to close a tag such as `<img src="image.jpg" alt="Image"`, the validator will alert you that the `<img>` tag is not self-closed. The corrected version would be:

```
<img src="image.jpg" alt="Image" />
```

3. Ensure Proper Structure

A valid XHTML document must have a proper structure, which includes:

- **DOCTYPE declaration:** The document must include the correct `<!DOCTYPE>` declaration for the version of XHTML you are using. For example:

```
<!DOCTYPE html PUBLIC "-//W3C//DTD XHTML 1.0 Strict//EN"
"http://www.w3.org/TR/xhtml1/DTD/xhtml1-strict.dtd">
```

This declaration specifies that the document follows the XHTML 1.0 Strict DTD (Document Type Definition).

- **XML Namespace in the `<html>` tag:** The `xmlns` attribute should be defined to specify the XML namespace for XHTML:

```
<html xmlns="http://www.w3.org/1999/xhtml">
```

- **Self-closing tags:** All void elements (e.g., `<img>`, `<br>`, `<hr>`) must be self-closed using a slash (`/`):

```
<img src="image.jpg" alt="An image" />
```

The W3C Validator checks these structural requirements and informs you if any of them are missing or incorrect.

---

4. Check for Compatibility

Once the code has been validated and fixed, it's important to ensure that the XHTML document is compatible with the devices and browsers you're targeting. XHTML is stricter than HTML, and some browsers may not render it correctly if it is not well-formed.

Common Compatibility Issues:

- **Browser Support for XHTML:** While most modern browsers support XHTML, some older versions or non-mainstream browsers may fail to render an XHTML page correctly if it doesn't follow the strict syntax rules.
- **MIME Type:** XHTML documents should be served with the correct MIME type (`application/xhtml+xml`) rather than the more common `text/html`. Serving XHTML with the wrong MIME type can cause it to be treated as HTML by some browsers, which can lead to incorrect rendering.

To prevent compatibility issues:

- **Test in Multiple Browsers:** Test the XHTML document in different browsers to ensure it displays correctly.
- **Validate Against Different Devices:** Ensure the page renders well on mobile devices or screen readers if accessibility is important.

Example of an Invalid XHTML Document

Here's an example of an invalid XHTML document:

```
<html>
  <head>
    <title>Invalid XHTML Page</title>
  </head>
  <body>
    <h1>Welcome</h1>
    <img src="image.jpg" alt="An image"  <!-- Missing the self-closing / -->
  </body>
</html>
```

Problem:

- The `<img>` tag is not properly closed. It should be written as `<img src="image.jpg" alt="An image" />` instead of `<img src="image.jpg" alt="An image">`.

Solution:
```
<html xmlns="http://www.w3.org/1999/xhtml">
  <head>
    <title>Valid XHTML Page</title>
  </head>
  <body>
    <h1>Welcome</h1>
    <img src="image.jpg" alt="An image" />
  </body>
</html>
```

- In the corrected version, the `<img>` tag is properly self-closed using `/>`.

In conclusion, XHTML provides a more rigorous structure for web pages compared to traditional HTML. It enforces strict rules on syntax, element nesting, and case sensitivity, making it more reliable for accessibility and cross-platform consistency. However, the advent of HTML5, which combines flexibility with modern web standards, has largely overtaken XHTML in most web development projects.

35 multiple-choice questions (MCQs)

1. What is XHTML?

- a) A programming language
- b) A stricter version of HTML based on XML
- c) A browser
- d) A web development tool

Answer: b) A stricter version of HTML based on XML

2. What is the key difference between XHTML and HTML?

- a) XHTML is more flexible than HTML
- b) XHTML is based on XML and follows strict syntax rules
- c) XHTML does not require the use of tags
- d) HTML is used only for text documents

Answer: b) XHTML is based on XML and follows strict syntax rules

3. Which of the following is required in XHTML but not in HTML?

- a) Self-closing tags
- b) Lowercase tags and attributes
- c) <html> tag
- d) <head> tag

Answer: b) Lowercase tags and attributes

4. What must every XHTML tag have?

- a) Only an opening tag
- b) Only a closing tag
- c) Both opening and closing tags
- d) No tags at all

Answer: c) Both opening and closing tags

5. In XHTML, which of the following is correct for an image tag?

- a) `<img src="image.jpg" alt="image">`
- b) `<img src="image.jpg" alt="image" />`
- c) `<img src=image.jpg alt=image>`
- d) `<image src="image.jpg" alt="image">`

Answer: b) `<img src="image.jpg" alt="image" />`

---

6. Which document type declaration (DOCTYPE) is used for XHTML 1.0 Strict?

- a) `<!DOCTYPE html>`
- b) `<!DOCTYPE XHTML>`
- c) `<!DOCTYPE html PUBLIC "-//W3C//DTD XHTML 1.0 Strict//EN" "http://www.w3.org/TR/xhtml1/DTD/xhtml1-strict.dtd">`
- d) `<!DOCTYPE html PUBLIC "html" "xhtml.dtd">`

Answer: c) `<!DOCTYPE html PUBLIC "-//W3C//DTD XHTML 1.0 Strict//EN" "http://www.w3.org/TR/xhtml1/DTD/xhtml1-strict.dtd">`

---

7. What is the xmlns attribute in the <html> tag used for in XHTML?

- a) Specifies the document type
- b) Specifies the character encoding
- c) Defines the XML namespace
- d) Defines the title of the document

Answer: c) Defines the XML namespace

---

8. What is required for an XHTML document to be considered well-formed?

- a) Properly nested tags
- b) Self-closing tags without a slash
- c) Only opening tags without closing tags
- d) Case-insensitive tag names

Answer: a) Properly nested tags

---

9. Which of the following elements should always be self-closed in XHTML?

- a) <img>
- b) <div>
- c) <p>
- d) <header>

Answer: a) <img>

10. Which of these elements requires an explicit closing tag in XHTML?

- a)
- b) <hr>
- c) <p>
- d) <img>

Answer: c) <p>

11. In XHTML, which of the following is incorrect syntax?

- a) `<input type="text" />`
- b) `<a href="link.html">Link</a>`
- c) `<div><h1>Title</h1></div>`
- d) `<br>`

Answer: d) `<br>` (It should be `<br />` in XHTML)

12. What is a requirement of all attributes in XHTML?

- a) They must be written in uppercase
- b) They must have a default value
- c) They must be enclosed in quotation marks
- d) They can be omitted

Answer: c) They must be enclosed in quotation marks

13. Which of the following tags is required to specify the character encoding in an XHTML document?

- a) `<meta charset="UTF-8" />`
- b) `<meta type="UTF-8" />`
- c) `<meta content="UTF-8" />`
- d) `<meta http-equiv="Content-Type" />`

Answer: a) `<meta charset="UTF-8" />`

14. Which of the following is true about XHTML documents?

- a) They are always backward-compatible with older browsers
- b) They must be well-formed to be processed by XML parsers
- c) They do not require a DOCTYPE declaration
- d) They do not allow external resources like stylesheets

Answer: b) They must be well-formed to be processed by XML parsers

15. Which of the following is the correct DOCTYPE declaration for an XHTML document?

- a) `<!DOCTYPE html>`
- b) `<!DOCTYPE xhtml>`
- c) `<!DOCTYPE html PUBLIC "html5">`
- d) `<!DOCTYPE html PUBLIC "-//W3C//DTD XHTML 1.0 Strict//EN" "http://www.w3.org/TR/xhtml1/DTD/xhtml1-strict.dtd">`

Answer: d) `<!DOCTYPE html PUBLIC "-//W3C//DTD XHTML 1.0 Strict//EN" "http://www.w3.org/TR/xhtml1/DTD/xhtml1-strict.dtd">`

16. Which of the following is true regarding void elements in XHTML?

- a) They do not require a closing tag
- b) They must have an opening and closing tag
- c) They must be self-closing using a slash (`/>`)
- d) They must have an opening tag only

Answer: c) They must be self-closing using a slash (`/>`)

17. What happens if an XHTML document is not well-formed?

- a) It will still display correctly in most browsers
- b) It will be ignored by browsers
- c) The document will fail to render properly in browsers supporting XML
- d) It will automatically correct itself

Answer: c) The document will fail to render properly in browsers supporting XML

---

18. Which of the following is a valid way to close an `<img>` tag in XHTML?

- a) `<img src="image.jpg" alt="An image">`
- b) `<img src="image.jpg" alt="An image" />`
- c) `<img src="image.jpg" alt="An image">/`
- d) `<image src="image.jpg" alt="An image" />`

Answer: b) `<img src="image.jpg" alt="An image" />`

---

19. Which element requires both opening and closing tags in XHTML?

- a) `<br>`
- b) `<img>`
- c) `<p>`
- d) `<hr>`

Answer: c) `<p>`

---

20. How can XHTML documents be validated?

- a) Using the W3C Validator tool
- b) Using a browser's developer tools
- c) By manually checking each tag
- d) By submitting it to a third-party vendor

Answer: a) Using the W3C Validator tool

21. Which of the following is required for an XHTML document to be well-formed?

- a) Tags should be written in uppercase
- b) Only opening tags are required
- c) Tags must be properly nested and closed
- d) External scripts are not allowed

Answer: c) Tags must be properly nested and closed

---

22. Which of the following is a feature of XHTML compared to HTML?

- a) It is less strict in terms of tag closure
- b) It requires all elements to be properly closed
- c) It allows missing end tags
- d) It does not support external CSS files

Answer: b) It requires all elements to be properly closed

---

23. What does the W3C Validator check for in an XHTML document?

- a) Correct use of CSS styles
- b) Well-formed syntax and correct tag structure
- c) JavaScript functionality
- d) Text content formatting

Answer: b) Well-formed syntax and correct tag structure

---

24. What is the primary reason for using XHTML instead of HTML?

- a) To allow greater flexibility in syntax
- b) To ensure stricter document structure and compatibility with XML
- c) To create mobile-only web applications
- d) To support older browsers

Answer: b) To ensure stricter document structure and compatibility with XML

25. In XHTML, which of the following is the correct way to declare the character set?

- a) `<meta charset=UTF-8 />`
- b) `<meta http-equiv="Content-Type" content="text/html; charset=UTF-8" />`
- c) `<meta type="UTF-8" />`
- d) `<meta charset="UTF-8">`

Answer: b) `<meta http-equiv="Content-Type" content="text/html; charset=UTF-8" />`

---

26. What is the function of the `xmlns` attribute in the `<html>` tag in XHTML?

- a) To specify the language of the document
- b) To declare the document type
- c) To specify the XML namespace for the document
- d) To specify the version of XHTML being used

Answer: c) To specify the XML namespace for the document

---

27. Which of the following is the correct way to close an empty element in XHTML?

- a) `<br>`
- b) `<br />`
- c) `<br></br>`
- d) `<br><br>`

Answer: b) `<br />`

---

28. Which tag requires proper closure in XHTML?

- a) `<br>`
- b) `<img>`
- c) `<a>`
- d) `<hr>`

Answer: c) `<a>`

29. What does an XHTML document require in comparison to HTML?

- a) It must use lowercase letters for all tags and attributes
- b) It uses a different character set
- c) It does not allow self-closing tags
- d) It must have an HTML5 declaration

Answer: a) It must use lowercase letters for all tags and attributes

---

30. How can a developer check whether their XHTML document is valid?

- a) By running the document in multiple browsers
- b) By using the W3C Validator to check the document for errors
- c) By checking for syntax highlighting in an editor
- d) By manually reviewing each line of code

Answer: b) By using the W3C Validator to check the document for errors

---

31. Which of the following must be properly handled in an XHTML document?

- a) Missing DOCTYPE
- b) Improper tag nesting
- c) External CSS links
- d) JavaScript functionality

Answer: b) Improper tag nesting

---

32. Which of the following is a feature of XHTML compared to HTML?

- a) XHTML is less strict about tag closure
- b) XHTML uses case-insensitive tags
- c) XHTML requires well-formed documents
- d) XHTML is deprecated for all modern web pages

Answer: c) XHTML requires well-formed documents

33. Which tag is required to specify that an XHTML document is using UTF-8 encoding?

- a) `<meta charset="UTF-8" />`
- b) `<meta http-equiv="Content-Type" content="text/html; charset=UTF-8" />`
- c) `<meta type="UTF-8" />`
- d) `<meta charset="utf-8">`

Answer: b) `<meta http-equiv="Content-Type" content="text/html; charset=UTF-8" />`

34. Why is XHTML considered more restrictive than HTML?

- a) It does not support multimedia content
- b) It requires all elements to be properly closed and formatted according to XML rules
- c) It only allows simple document structures
- d) It removes the need for CSS

Answer: b) It requires all elements to be properly closed and formatted according to XML rules

35. Which tag requires a self-closing slash (/) in XHTML?

- a) `<br>`
- b) `<div>`
- c) `<p>`
- d) `<head>`

Answer: a) `<br>`

25 short questions and answers

1. What is XHTML?

- **Answer:** XHTML (Extensible Hypertext Markup Language) is a stricter version of HTML that follows XML syntax rules.

2. How is XHTML different from HTML?

- **Answer:** XHTML is more strict, requiring proper tag closure, lowercase tags, and a well-formed structure, while HTML is more forgiving.

3. What does "well-formed" mean in the context of XHTML?

- **Answer:** A well-formed document follows XML rules, including properly nested and closed tags, and properly quoted attribute values.

4. What is the main advantage of using XHTML?

- **Answer:** XHTML ensures cleaner, more structured code that is easier to maintain and more compatible with XML parsers.

5. What is the document type declaration for XHTML 1.0 Strict?

- **Answer:** `<!DOCTYPE html PUBLIC "-//W3C//DTD XHTML 1.0 Strict//EN" "http://www.w3.org/TR/xhtml1/DTD/xhtml1-strict.dtd">`

6. What does the `xmlns` attribute in the `<html>` tag define in XHTML?

- **Answer:** The `xmlns` attribute defines the XML namespace for the document.

7. Why must tags be written in lowercase in XHTML?

- **Answer:** XHTML requires tags and attributes to be case-sensitive, with all tags written in lowercase to comply with XML standards.

8. What must every element in XHTML have?

- **Answer:** Every element in XHTML must have both an opening and a closing tag, except for self-closing tags.

9. How do you self-close an element like `<img>` in XHTML?

- **Answer:** By adding a slash at the end: `<img src="image.jpg" alt="description" />`

---

10. What happens if an XHTML document is not well-formed?

- **Answer:** If not well-formed, the document may not render properly in browsers supporting XML.

---

11. What is required in XHTML but not in HTML regarding tag closure?

- **Answer:** XHTML requires explicit closure of all tags, including self-closing ones like `<img>` and `<br>`.

---

12. What is the role of the DOCTYPE declaration in an XHTML document?

- **Answer:** The `DOCTYPE` declaration specifies the XHTML version being used and helps browsers render the page correctly.

---

13. Which tag in XHTML requires a self-closing slash (/)?

- **Answer:** Tags like `<br>`, `<img>`, and `<hr>` require a self-closing slash in XHTML.

---

14. In XHTML, how are attributes written?

- **Answer:** Attributes must be written in lowercase and enclosed in quotation marks, e.g., `src="image.jpg"`.

---

15. Why is XHTML considered more strict than HTML?

- **Answer:** XHTML is strict about syntax, requiring proper tag closure, correct nesting, and lowercase attributes.

16. What should you do if an XHTML document does not pass validation?

- **Answer:** You need to fix syntax errors, such as missing tags or improper nesting, to ensure the document is valid.

---

17. How can you validate an XHTML document?

- **Answer:** You can use the W3C Markup Validation Service to check if the document adheres to XHTML standards.

---

18. What is required for an XHTML document to be considered valid?

- **Answer:** It must be well-formed, with properly closed tags, correct attribute syntax, and a valid `DOCTYPE` declaration.

---

19. What is the purpose of validating XHTML code?

- **Answer:** Validation ensures the document follows XHTML rules, improving accessibility, rendering consistency, and error detection.

---

20. What happens if a self-closing tag like `<img>` is not properly closed in XHTML?

- **Answer:** The document will fail to pass validation and may not render correctly in XML-compatible browsers.

---

21. What is the function of the `<meta charset="UTF-8" />` tag in XHTML?

- **Answer:** It specifies the character encoding of the document, ensuring proper display of special characters.

---

22. What must be done to ensure proper nesting of tags in XHTML?

- **Answer:** Tags must be properly opened and closed in the correct order, with no elements left unclosed or improperly nested.

---

23. Which tool is commonly used to validate XHTML code?

- **Answer:** The W3C Markup Validation Service is commonly used to validate XHTML code.

---

24. Can an XHTML document be rendered in a browser that supports XML if it is not well-formed?

- **Answer:** No, an improperly formed XHTML document will not render correctly in XML-compliant browsers.

---

25. What does the `meta` tag in XHTML usually contain?

- **Answer:** The `meta` tag typically contains metadata such as the document's character encoding, author information, and page description.

CHAPTER 3: DYNAMIC HTML (DHTML)

What is DHTML and Why It's Useful?

DHTML (Dynamic HTML) is a term that refers to a set of technologies used together to make web pages interactive and dynamic. Unlike traditional static HTML, which presents content that remains unchanged until a page is reloaded, DHTML allows web content to be manipulated dynamically on the client side—without requiring the entire page to refresh. This is achieved by combining several technologies:

1. **HTML (HyperText Markup Language):** The standard markup language used to structure the content on the web page (text, images, links, etc.).
2. **CSS (Cascading Style Sheets):** Used to control the layout, styling, and visual presentation of web elements.
3. **JavaScript:** A programming language that allows you to interact with the page elements and manipulate them dynamically.
4. **DOM (Document Object Model):** An API that provides an interface for JavaScript to access and modify the structure, content, and style of a webpage.

The key feature of DHTML is that it allows the manipulation of the content and styling of web pages in real-time based on user interactions, such as mouse movements, clicks, or keyboard inputs.

Why is DHTML Useful?

DHTML offers a range of benefits that help improve the interactivity, user experience, and performance of websites. Below are the key reasons why DHTML is useful:

1. Interactivity

- DHTML enables real-time interactivity, allowing web pages to respond to various user actions without having to reload the page. For example:
    - Clicking on an element to change its content or appearance.
    - Hovering over a button to trigger a visual effect or show additional information.
    - Typing in a form field that dynamically suggests input based on user actions (e.g., autocompletion).

These dynamic interactions make websites more engaging and intuitive, fostering a more responsive user experience.

Example:

- A drop-down menu that appears when the user hovers over a navigation item, or a form that provides live validation of user input.

2. Enhanced User Experience

- DHTML helps create a smoother and more seamless user experience by reducing the need to reload pages. This not only speeds up interactions but also makes the website feel more responsive and modern.
- For example, instead of a full page reload when a user clicks on a button to view more information, DHTML can dynamically update the content in place without interrupting the user's flow.

Example:

- A live search feature where search results update instantly as the user types, or interactive maps that allow users to zoom and pan smoothly without page reloads.

3. Reduced Server Load

- Traditionally, dynamic web content requires constant communication with the server. Each time a user interacts with a page, the server must process the request, send data back, and reload the page. This can put a significant load on the server, especially with high-traffic websites.
- DHTML reduces the load on the server by shifting many of the content manipulations to the client-side. This means the server only needs to send data once, and the client (browser) takes over to handle real-time updates and interactions.

Example:

- Instead of sending a request to the server every time a user clicks a button to update content, DHTML can use JavaScript to directly manipulate the page's content in the browser.

4. Efficient for Creating Dynamic Web Content

- DHTML empowers developers to create sophisticated dynamic content such as animations, real-time updates, interactive forms, and rich user interfaces. This flexibility allows websites to go beyond basic, static pages and create more engaging, interactive, and visually appealing experiences.
- With DHTML, developers can manipulate not only content (like text and images) but also styles (like colors, sizes, or positions) and behaviors (like animations or event responses) in real time.

Example:

- Interactive elements like collapsible sections, image sliders, and drag-and-drop interfaces can all be created with DHTML.

Key Use Cases of DHTML

DHTML (Dynamic HTML) is particularly valuable for creating rich, interactive, and dynamic web experiences. Here are some detailed key use cases where DHTML shines:

1. Dynamic Navigation

- **What It Is:**
  Dynamic navigation refers to menus and navigation systems that adapt and change based on user interactions. These menus might expand, collapse, slide, or show additional content as users hover over or click on specific items.
- **Why It's Useful:**
  - **Space Efficiency:** Dynamic menus can save valuable screen real estate by showing more options only when necessary.
  - **User Engagement:** Interactive menus create a more engaging and visually appealing user experience.
  - **Simplified User Interaction:** Users can easily access more content without navigating away from the page or reloading the site.
- **How It Works with DHTML:** DHTML allows navigation systems to change their appearance and behavior in real-time using JavaScript and CSS. This is done by manipulating the CSS properties like `display`, `visibility`, `position`, and `opacity`.
- **Example:** A **drop-down menu** that appears when the user hovers over a main menu item, or a **flyout menu** that shows additional options when a user clicks a menu link. Both of these elements can be dynamically created and controlled using DHTML.

```
<ul>
  <li><a href="#">Home</a></li>
  <li><a href="#">About</a></li>
  <li><a href="#">Services</a>
    <ul>
      <li><a href="#">Web Design</a></li>
      <li><a href="#">SEO</a></li>
    </ul>
  </li>
</ul>
<style>
  ul ul { display: none; }
  li:hover > ul { display: block; }
</style>
```

- **Example in Practice:**
  Websites like Amazon and eBay use expanding and collapsing menus to organize their categories, making navigation easier and more intuitive.

2. Form Validation

- **What It Is:**
  Form validation ensures that user input is accurate and formatted correctly before submitting a form. With DHTML, forms can be validated dynamically without requiring a page reload, offering immediate feedback to users.
- **Why It's Useful:**
  - **Real-Time Feedback:** Users are informed of errors as they type or interact with form fields, reducing frustration and preventing invalid form submissions.
  - **Better User Experience:** Form validation via DHTML eliminates the need for a round-trip to the server, providing a smoother experience.
  - **Error Prevention:** With client-side validation, obvious errors (such as missing required fields or incorrect formats) can be caught before submission.
- **How It Works with DHTML:** DHTML uses JavaScript to validate form input dynamically. JavaScript is used to listen for user actions like onblur (when the user moves out of an input field) or onsubmit (when the form is submitted), then checks the validity of the input fields.
- **Example:** A **username field** that checks if the entered username meets the minimum length requirement as the user types.

```
function validateForm() {
  var username = document.getElementById("username").value;
  if (username.length < 6) {
    alert("Username must be at least 6 characters.");
    return false;
  }
  return true;
}
```

- **Example in Practice:**
  Sites like Facebook or Gmail show dynamic error messages for things like incorrect email formats or password length issues instantly as users interact with form fields.

---

3. Live Content Updates

- **What It Is:**
  Live content updates refer to websites displaying dynamic information that updates in real time without requiring the entire page to refresh. This is often used for displaying live data such as stock prices, social media feeds, or news headlines.
- **Why It's Useful:**
  - **Instant Information:** Users can get the most up-to-date content without refreshing the page.
  - **Improved Engagement:** Real-time updates keep users engaged and informed.
  - **Efficiency:** Reduces the need for full-page reloads, thus providing a more fluid and faster browsing experience.

- **How It Works with DHTML:** Using DHTML, JavaScript can request data from a server (often via AJAX) and update the content of a page without a full refresh. The DOM is updated with the new data, and CSS can be used to animate the changes (e.g., smoothly adding new content).
- **Example:** A **live stock ticker** that automatically updates prices every few seconds.

```
setInterval(function() {
  document.getElementById("stockPrice").innerText = "Price: $" +
getNewStockPrice();
}, 5000);
```

- **Example in Practice:**
  Websites like Twitter, Facebook, and CNN use live content updates to refresh feeds and display new posts or headlines without requiring the user to reload the page.

4. Interactive Widgets

- **What It Is:**
  Interactive widgets are dynamic, interactive components embedded within a webpage that respond to user actions. These can include elements like image galleries, slideshows, interactive maps, or video players. They allow users to interact with the page in creative and engaging ways.
- **Why It's Useful:**
  - **Enhanced Engagement:** Widgets keep users involved in the content and encourage them to interact with the page.
  - **Rich Media Integration:** Widgets like image sliders or video players create a visually appealing experience and can be integrated with multimedia content.
  - **Ease of Use:** Interactive elements provide more intuitive ways to access and explore content.
- **How It Works with DHTML:** Interactive widgets rely heavily on JavaScript to handle user events (like clicks, hover actions, or keyboard inputs). JavaScript manipulates the DOM to change the widget's behavior or appearance in response to these events.
- **Example:** An **image slider** that lets users click "Next" and "Previous" buttons to navigate through a set of images.

```
<div class="slider">
  <button onclick="prevImage()">Prev</button>
  <img id="slide" src="image1.jpg" />
  <button onclick="nextImage()">Next</button>
</div>

<script>
  let currentImage = 0;
  const images = ["image1.jpg", "image2.jpg", "image3.jpg"];
  function prevImage() {
    currentImage = (currentImage === 0) ? images.length - 1 :
currentImage - 1;
```

```
    document.getElementById("slide").src = images[currentImage];
  }
  function nextImage() {
    currentImage = (currentImage === images.length - 1) ? 0 :
currentImage + 1;
    document.getElementById("slide").src = images[currentImage];
  }
</script>
```

- **Example in Practice:**
  Websites like Instagram or Pinterest feature interactive image galleries that allow users to click through photos, zoom in, or swipe between images seamlessly. Additionally, YouTube and Vimeo use interactive video players with play, pause, volume controls, and captions.

Adding Interactivity to Web Pages with DHTML

Dynamic HTML (DHTML) is a powerful tool for enhancing web pages by making them interactive and responsive to user actions in real time, without requiring a page reload. By manipulating HTML elements, CSS styles, and JavaScript, developers can create dynamic content that responds to user interactions, leading to a more engaging and fluid user experience.

Here, we will break down how interactivity is added to web pages with DHTML, focusing on three key aspects: **Mouse Events**, **User Input**, and **Real-time Changes**.

1. Mouse Events

Mouse events allow developers to detect and respond to various actions performed by users on a webpage, such as mouse movements, clicks, hover states, etc. With DHTML, these events can trigger dynamic content changes, making the web page feel more interactive.

Types of Mouse Events:

- **onmouseover:** Triggered when the mouse pointer moves over an element.
- **onmouseout:** Triggered when the mouse pointer moves out of an element.
- **onclick:** Triggered when the user clicks on an element.
- **ondblclick:** Triggered when the user double-clicks on an element.
- **mousemove:** Triggered when the mouse moves within an element.
- **mousedown / mouseup:** Triggered when a mouse button is pressed or released.

Example: Hovering over an image to change its appearance

In DHTML, we can use JavaScript to detect mouse events like hovering and modify elements dynamically. For instance, we might change the background color of a button when the user hovers over it, or enlarge an image.

```html
<!DOCTYPE html>
<html lang="en">
<head>
    <meta charset="UTF-8">
    <title>Mouse Event Example</title>
    <style>
        #hoverButton {
            padding: 10px 20px;
            background-color: lightblue;
            border: none;
            cursor: pointer;
        }
    </style>
</head>
<body>

<button id="hoverButton" onmouseover="changeColor()"
onmouseout="resetColor()">Hover over me</button>

<script>
    function changeColor() {
        document.getElementById("hoverButton").style.backgroundColor =
"green";
    }

    function resetColor() {
        document.getElementById("hoverButton").style.backgroundColor =
"lightblue";
    }
</script>

</body>
</html>
```

In this example, when the user hovers over the button, the onmouseover event triggers the changeColor() function, which changes the button's background color to green. When the user moves the mouse away, the onmouseout event triggers the resetColor() function to restore the original color.

2. User Input

User input can be gathered from form fields like text boxes, radio buttons, and checkboxes. By processing this input dynamically, we can update the page's content in real-time, without requiring the user to submit the form or refresh the page.

Types of User Input:

- **Text input fields:** Users type into fields like `<input>` or `<textarea>`.
- **Select dropdowns:** Users select options from a dropdown list.
- **Radio buttons/Checkboxes:** Users make selections by clicking on radio buttons or checkboxes.
- **Submit buttons:** Users submit forms with input data.

Example: Real-time form validation

One of the most common ways to use DHTML for user input is real-time form validation. As the user enters data into a field, JavaScript can instantly validate whether the input is correct and provide feedback, all without reloading the page.

```
<!DOCTYPE html>
<html lang="en">
<head>
    <meta charset="UTF-8">
    <title>Real-Time Form Validation</title>
    <style>
        .valid {
            color: green;
        }
        .invalid {
            color: red;
        }
    </style>
</head>
<body>

<form>
    <label for="email">Email:</label>
    <input type="text" id="email" oninput="validateEmail()" />
    <span id="emailFeedback"></span>
</form>

<script>
    function validateEmail() {
        var email = document.getElementById("email").value;
        var feedback = document.getElementById("emailFeedback");
        var regex = /^[a-zA-Z0-9._-]+@[a-zA-Z0-9.-]+\.[a-zA-Z]{2,6}$/;

        if (regex.test(email)) {
            feedback.textContent = "Valid email address!";
            feedback.className = "valid";
        } else {
            feedback.textContent = "Invalid email address!";
            feedback.className = "invalid";
        }
    }
</script>

</body>
</html>
```

In this example, as the user types an email address, the `oninput` event is triggered, calling the `validateEmail()` function. The function uses a regular expression to check the email format and provides instant feedback (valid or invalid) beside the field.

---

3. Real-time Changes

Real-time changes refer to the ability to update page content or appearance based on user actions or other events. This could involve dynamically showing or hiding elements, changing the styles (e.g., colors or sizes), or adjusting layouts based on interactions.

Example: Toggle visibility of an element

One common use case for DHTML is the ability to show or hide elements based on user interaction. This can be particularly useful for things like collapsible menus, expanding sections, or modals that display when triggered by a button or link.

```html
<!DOCTYPE html>
<html lang="en">
<head>
    <meta charset="UTF-8">
    <title>Toggle Visibility</title>
    <style>
        #content {
            display: none;
            background-color: lightgrey;
            padding: 20px;
        }
    </style>
</head>
<body>

<button onclick="toggleVisibility()">Toggle Content</button>
<div id="content">
    <p>This content is dynamically shown or hidden based on user action.</p>
</div>

<script>
    function toggleVisibility() {
        var content = document.getElementById("content");
        if (content.style.display === "none") {
            content.style.display = "block";
        } else {
            content.style.display = "none";
        }
    }
</script>

</body>
</html>
```

In this example, clicking the "Toggle Content" button triggers the `toggleVisibility()` function, which toggles the `display` property of the `#content` element. When the content is hidden, clicking the button will show it; when it's visible, clicking the button will hide it.

Example: Changing the background color

Another example is changing the background color of the page or any element based on user actions, such as mouse movements, clicks, or form selections.

```
<!DOCTYPE html>
<html lang="en">
<head>
    <meta charset="UTF-8">
    <title>Change Background Color</title>
</head>
<body>

<button onclick="changeColor()">Click to Change Background Color</button>

<script>
    function changeColor() {
        document.body.style.backgroundColor = "lightcoral";
    }
</script>

</body>
</html>
```

In this case, the background color of the page changes when the user clicks the button. This is done by directly manipulating the page's CSS using JavaScript.

.

Understanding CSS, JavaScript, and the DOM (Document Object Model)

For **DHTML (Dynamic HTML)** to function effectively and dynamically change the content and presentation of a web page, three core technologies need to work together: **CSS (Cascading Style Sheets)**, **JavaScript**, and the **DOM (Document Object Model)**. Let's explore each of these components in detail and see how they work together to create dynamic, interactive web pages.

1. CSS (Cascading Style Sheets)

What is CSS?

CSS is a stylesheet language used to control the presentation of a web page. It defines how HTML elements are displayed on the screen, including aspects like layout, colors, fonts, spacing, positioning, and visibility.

Role of CSS in DHTML:

In the context of DHTML, **CSS** is responsible for the visual appearance and layout of elements on the page. One of the key features of DHTML is its ability to **dynamically manipulate the CSS properties** of elements based on user interactions (such as mouseovers, clicks, or keyboard input). This allows for dynamic changes in the appearance of the page without needing to reload or refresh the entire document.

With DHTML, JavaScript interacts with the CSS properties in real-time, allowing developers to change things like:

- **Colors** (background, text, borders)
- **Visibility** (show/hide elements)
- **Positioning** (move elements around the screen)
- **Size** (resize elements)
- **Display properties** (e.g., `block`, `inline`, `none`)

Example: Using JavaScript to modify a button's background color

Here's a simple example that uses JavaScript to change a button's background color dynamically when the user hovers over it. The CSS defines the default style, and JavaScript modifies the style in response to the user's actions.

```
<!DOCTYPE html>
<html lang="en">
<head>
    <meta charset="UTF-8">
    <title>CSS and JavaScript Example</title>
    <style>
        #myButton {
            padding: 10px 20px;
            background-color: lightblue;
            border: 2px solid blue;
            cursor: pointer;
        }
    </style>
</head>
<body>

<button id="myButton" onmouseover="changeColor()"
onmouseout="resetColor()">Hover over me</button>
```

```
<script>
    function changeColor() {
        document.getElementById("myButton").style.backgroundColor = "green";
    }

    function resetColor() {
        document.getElementById("myButton").style.backgroundColor =
"lightblue";
    }
</script>

</body>
</html>
```

In this example:

- **CSS** is used to initially style the button (background-color, padding, border).
- **JavaScript** listens for the mouseover and mouseout events to dynamically change the background-color of the button when the user interacts with it.

---

2. JavaScript

What is JavaScript?

JavaScript is a high-level, dynamic programming language that enables interactive web pages. It is used to manipulate HTML and CSS, making web pages more responsive to user actions. With JavaScript, developers can respond to events (like clicks, mouse movements, keypresses) and modify the content or style of web pages in real-time.

Role of JavaScript in DHTML:

In DHTML, JavaScript is the core programming language that enables dynamic behavior. JavaScript interacts with HTML elements and CSS styles to:

- **Manipulate HTML structure:** Create, modify, or delete HTML elements (like div, button, image).
- **Change CSS styles:** Adjust the appearance of elements dynamically (like changing color, size, position).
- **Handle user interactions:** Respond to mouse events (e.g., onclick, onmouseover), keyboard events (e.g., onkeyup, onkeydown), or form input (e.g., validation).
- **Create animations:** Animate transitions or move elements across the screen.

JavaScript can also be used to **validate forms**, **create interactive features**, and perform **AJAX requests** for live content updates without reloading the page.

Example: Creating an animation with JavaScript

Here's an example that uses JavaScript to animate an element, making it move across the screen when a button is clicked.

```
<!DOCTYPE html>
<html lang="en">
<head>
    <meta charset="UTF-8">
    <title>JavaScript Animation</title>
    <style>
        #movingElement {
            width: 100px;
            height: 100px;
            background-color: blue;
            position: absolute;
            left: 0;
        }
    </style>
</head>
<body>

<button onclick="moveElement()">Move Element</button>
<div id="movingElement"></div>

<script>
    function moveElement() {
        var element = document.getElementById("movingElement");
        var left = 0;

        var interval = setInterval(function() {
            if (left < 500) {
                left += 5;
                element.style.left = left + "px";
            } else {
                clearInterval(interval); // Stop moving once it reaches 500px
            }
        }, 20); // Move element every 20 milliseconds
    }
</script>

</body>
</html>
```

In this example:

- **JavaScript** is used to animate the `div` with the ID `movingElement`.
- The `setInterval` function repeatedly moves the element by increasing its `left` position, creating an animation effect.

3. DOM (Document Object Model)

What is the DOM?

The **Document Object Model (DOM)** is a programming interface that represents the structure of an HTML or XML document as a tree of nodes. Each node in the DOM tree corresponds to an HTML element or attribute. The DOM allows JavaScript to access and manipulate the content and structure of a web page in real time.

The DOM represents the entire structure of the page as a hierarchical tree of objects. The **document** is the root of the tree, and all HTML elements (such as `<div>`, `<h1>`, `<p>`) are nodes in that tree.

Role of the DOM in DHTML:

The DOM allows **JavaScript** to:

- **Access elements:** JavaScript can select HTML elements using methods like `getElementById`, `getElementsByClassName`, `querySelector`, etc.
- **Modify content:** JavaScript can change the inner content of an element (like the text inside a `div` or the `src` of an image).
- **Manipulate attributes:** JavaScript can change HTML attributes (e.g., `href`, `src`, `alt`).
- **Change structure:** JavaScript can add, remove, or modify elements in the DOM (e.g., appending new elements or removing existing ones).

Example: Changing the content of a `<div>` using the DOM

Here's an example that demonstrates how to use JavaScript and the DOM to change the text inside a `div` element dynamically.

```
<!DOCTYPE html>
<html lang="en">
<head>
    <meta charset="UTF-8">
    <title>DOM Manipulation Example</title>
</head>
<body>

<div id="myDiv">Original Text</div>
<button onclick="changeText()">Change Text</button>

<script>
    function changeText() {
        // Access the div element using its ID and change its text
        document.getElementById("myDiv").innerHTML = "New Text!";
    }
</script>

</body>
</html>
```

In this example:

- **JavaScript** uses the DOM method `getElementById()` to select the `div` with the ID `myDiv`.
- The `innerHTML` property is used to change the content inside the `div` to "New Text!" when the user clicks the button.

Manipulating Page Elements Using DHTML

Manipulating page elements is a fundamental aspect of **DHTML (Dynamic HTML)**, allowing developers to create dynamic and interactive web pages. **JavaScript** is the key technology used to interact with **HTML elements** and modify their content, appearance, position, and visibility in real time. By leveraging the **DOM (Document Object Model)**, JavaScript can access and change properties of HTML elements to create a seamless and dynamic user experience. Below are some of the most common types of manipulations you can perform using DHTML.

1. Changing Element Content

One of the simplest and most common manipulations in DHTML is changing the content of an HTML element. You can dynamically update the text or HTML inside an element using JavaScript.

Example: Changing the inner HTML of an element

You can use the `innerHTML` property of an element to modify its content. This allows you to change the text or even insert new HTML elements into a specific container.

```
<!DOCTYPE html>
<html lang="en">
<head>
    <meta charset="UTF-8">
    <title>Change Element Content</title>
</head>
<body>

<div id="myDiv">Original content</div>
<button onclick="changeContent()">Change Content</button>

<script>
    function changeContent() {
        document.getElementById("myDiv").innerHTML = "New content has been
added!";
    }
</script>

</body>
</html>
```

In this example:

- When the user clicks the "Change Content" button, the `changeContent()` function is triggered.
- The `innerHTML` property of the `div` with `id="myDiv"` is updated, changing the text inside it to "New content has been added!".

Use Cases:

- Updating content based on user interactions (e.g., showing results of a form submission).
- Dynamically inserting new content such as images, links, or lists.

2. Modifying CSS Styles

In DHTML, you can modify the **CSS styles** of elements dynamically using JavaScript. This allows you to change the appearance of elements on the fly, based on user actions or other events.

Example: Changing an element's background color

You can dynamically modify an element's style properties, such as `backgroundColor`, `fontSize`, `width`, or `height`, using JavaScript. Here's an example of changing the background color of a `div` element:

```
<!DOCTYPE html>
<html lang="en">
<head>
    <meta charset="UTF-8">
    <title>Modify CSS Styles</title>
</head>
<body>

<div id="myDiv" style="width: 200px; height: 200px; background-color:
lightblue;">Click to change color</div>
<button onclick="changeColor()">Change Color</button>

<script>
    function changeColor() {
        document.getElementById("myDiv").style.backgroundColor = "green";
    }
</script>

</body>
</html>
```

In this example:

- The `div` starts with a light blue background color.

- When the "Change Color" button is clicked, the `changeColor()` function is executed, modifying the `backgroundColor` CSS property of the `div` to `green`.

Use Cases:

- Changing colors, borders, or fonts based on user interactions (e.g., hovering over a button).
- Animating elements by dynamically changing properties like width, height, or opacity.

3. Positioning Elements

You can also use JavaScript to change the **positioning** of an element on the page, either statically (e.g., by adjusting margins) or dynamically (e.g., by animating its movement).

Example: Changing an element's position using JavaScript

By manipulating the `style.position`, `style.top`, `style.left`, or `style.bottom` properties, you can move elements around the page.

```html
<!DOCTYPE html>
<html lang="en">
<head>
    <meta charset="UTF-8">
    <title>Position Element</title>
    <style>
        #myDiv {
            width: 100px;
            height: 100px;
            background-color: blue;
            position: absolute;
        }
    </style>
</head>
<body>

<button onclick="moveElement()">Move Element</button>
<div id="myDiv"></div>

<script>
    function moveElement() {
        document.getElementById("myDiv").style.left = "200px";   // Move to
the right
        document.getElementById("myDiv").style.top = "150px";    // Move down
    }
</script>

</body>
</html>
```

In this example:

- The `div` element starts in its default position (the top-left corner).
- When the "Move Element" button is clicked, the `moveElement()` function is executed, updating the `left` and `top` properties to move the `div` element 200px to the right and 150px down.

Use Cases:

- Creating animations where elements move across the screen.
- Making interactive elements that adjust based on user actions, such as dragging or resizing.

---

4. Showing/Hiding Elements

JavaScript allows you to show or hide elements dynamically by manipulating their **CSS `display`** or **`visibility`** properties. This can be useful for creating interactive features like dropdown menus, modals, or tooltips.

Example: Toggling visibility of an element

You can toggle the visibility of an element by modifying its `style.display` property. Setting `display` to `none` hides the element, and setting it to `block` or another appropriate value shows the element again.

```
<!DOCTYPE html>
<html lang="en">
<head>
    <meta charset="UTF-8">
    <title>Show/Hide Element</title>
</head>
<body>

<button onclick="toggleVisibility()">Toggle Visibility</button>
<div id="myDiv" style="width: 200px; height: 100px; background-color:
yellow;">This is a visible element</div>

<script>
    function toggleVisibility() {
        var element = document.getElementById("myDiv");
        if (element.style.display === "none") {
            element.style.display = "block"; // Show the element
        } else {
            element.style.display = "none"; // Hide the element
        }
    }
</script>

</body>
</html>
```

In this example:

- Initially, the `div` element is visible.
- When the user clicks the "Toggle Visibility" button, the `toggleVisibility()` function checks the current value of the `display` property.
  - If the `div` is visible, it sets `display` to `none` (hiding it).
  - If the `div` is hidden, it sets `display` to `block` (showing it).

Use Cases:

- Show or hide elements like forms, dialogs, or additional content based on user interaction.
- Create collapsible or expandable menus or sections on a webpage.

Animation and Effects with DHTML

DHTML (Dynamic HTML) is a powerful tool for creating dynamic and interactive animations and visual effects on web pages. By combining **JavaScript, CSS**, and the **DOM (Document Object Model)**, developers can animate page elements, create smooth transitions, and enhance the user experience.

In DHTML, you can achieve animation effects like **moving elements, fading in/out, color transitions**, and **sliding objects** across the page. Let's break down the different methods for creating animations and effects using DHTML.

1. Creating Animations with JavaScript

JavaScript allows you to create animations by updating the properties of elements over time. You can manipulate CSS properties (like `left`, `top`, `opacity`, etc.) within a loop or at intervals, which makes it possible to simulate movement, resizing, and other dynamic changes.

Example: Moving an Element Horizontally

One common animation is moving an element horizontally across the page. Using JavaScript, you can incrementally update the position of an element and create the illusion of smooth movement.

```
<!DOCTYPE html>
<html lang="en">
<head>
    <meta charset="UTF-8">
    <title>Move Element</title>
    <style>
        #myDiv {
```

```
            width: 100px;
            height: 100px;
            background-color: red;
            position: absolute;
            left: 0;
            top: 100px;
        }
    </style>
</head>
<body>

<div id="myDiv"></div>

<script>
    var elem = document.getElementById("myDiv");
    var pos = 0;

    function moveRight() {
        pos++;
        elem.style.left = pos + "px";  // Update the element's left position
        if (pos < 200) {
            requestAnimationFrame(moveRight); // Keep moving the element
until it reaches 200px
        }
    }

    moveRight();  // Start the animation
</script>

</body>
</html>
```
Explanation:

- **JavaScript** is used to move the `div` element from left to right.
- The `moveRight()` function increases the `left` position of the element by 1 pixel on each call.
- The **requestAnimationFrame()** method is used to ensure smooth animations by synchronizing them with the browser's repaint cycle, making the movement smooth.

Use Cases:

- Moving objects across the screen, such as sliding panels or images.
- Animating the movement of UI elements like buttons or icons when clicked or hovered.

---

2. CSS Transitions and Animations

While JavaScript provides more flexibility, **CSS** also offers powerful tools for creating animations and visual effects. **CSS transitions** allow you to smoothly transition between two states (e.g., changing from one background color to another), and **CSS animations** can animate an element over a sequence of keyframes.

A simple and common effect is to change an element's background color when the user hovers over it. With CSS transitions, this change can happen smoothly.

```
<!DOCTYPE html>
<html lang="en">
<head>
    <meta charset="UTF-8">
    <title>CSS Transition</title>
    <style>
        #myDiv {
            width: 200px;
            height: 200px;
            background-color: lightblue;
            transition: background-color 0.5s ease;  /* Define a smooth
transition */
        }

        #myDiv:hover {
            background-color: blue;  /* Change color on hover */
        }
    </style>
</head>
<body>

<div id="myDiv"></div>

</body>
</html>
```

Explanation:

- The `#myDiv` element has a `background-color` of light blue.
- The `transition` property tells the browser to animate the `background-color` over a duration of **0.5 seconds** with an **ease** timing function.
- When the user hovers over the `div`, the background color changes to blue with a smooth transition.

Use Cases:

- Hover effects, like changing colors or scaling an element.
- Smooth transitions for UI elements like buttons, links, or containers when the state changes.

---

3. CSS Animations (Keyframe Animations)

CSS Animations go beyond simple transitions and allow for more complex effects. Using **keyframes**, you can define specific points of an animation over time, giving you full control over the behavior of an element at different stages of the animation.

Example: Slide-in Animation Using Keyframes

This example animates an element to slide from the left to the center of the page.

```html
<!DOCTYPE html>
<html lang="en">
<head>
    <meta charset="UTF-8">
    <title>CSS Animation</title>
    <style>
        #myDiv {
            width: 100px;
            height: 100px;
            background-color: green;
            position: absolute;
            left: -150px;   /* Start off-screen */
            animation: slideIn 2s ease-in-out forwards;   /* Apply animation
*/
        }

        @keyframes slideIn {
            0% {
                left: -150px;   /* Start from the left */
            }
            100% {
                left: 50%;   /* End at the center */
                transform: translateX(-50%);   /* Adjust for centering */
            }
        }
    </style>
</head>
<body>

<div id="myDiv"></div>

</body>
</html>
```

Explanation:

- The `@keyframes` rule defines the animation named `slideIn`.
- The animation starts with `left: -150px` (off-screen to the left) and ends at `left: 50%` (the center of the page). The `transform: translateX(-50%)` centers the element exactly in the middle of the page.
- The animation is applied to the `#myDiv` element, which slides from left to right over **2 seconds** with an **ease-in-out** timing function.

Use Cases:

- Creating more complex animations like sliding panels, rotating elements, or fading effects.
- Animating elements based on user interaction (e.g., showing hidden content or sliding in a menu).

4. Combining JavaScript and CSS for Complex Effects

While CSS animations and transitions are great for many simple effects, **JavaScript** can add even more power and flexibility. By combining **JavaScript** with **CSS**, you can control animations, trigger events, and create highly interactive effects.

Example: Fading an Element In and Out

This example uses **JavaScript** to trigger a fade-in and fade-out effect by adjusting the **CSS** `opacity` property.

```
<!DOCTYPE html>
<html lang="en">
<head>
    <meta charset="UTF-8">
    <title>Fade In and Out</title>
    <style>
        #myDiv {
            width: 100px;
            height: 100px;
            background-color: orange;
            opacity: 0;  /* Start as invisible */
            transition: opacity 1s ease;  /* Apply a smooth fade transition */
        }
    </style>
</head>
<body>

<button onclick="fadeIn()">Fade In</button>
<button onclick="fadeOut()">Fade Out</button>
<div id="myDiv"></div>

<script>
    function fadeIn() {
        document.getElementById("myDiv").style.opacity = 1;  // Make the element visible
    }

    function fadeOut() {
        document.getElementById("myDiv").style.opacity = 0;  // Make the element invisible
    }
</script>

</body>
</html>
```

Explanation:

- Initially, the `div` has an `opacity` of 0, making it invisible.
- The `transition` property ensures that when the `opacity` changes, it does so smoothly over **1 second**.

- JavaScript functions `fadeIn()` and `fadeOut()` change the `opacity` to **1** (fully visible) or **0** (invisible), respectively.

Use Cases:

- Fade in/out for alerts, messages, or notifications.
- Smoothly showing or hiding elements (e.g., toggling visibility of modals, dropdowns, or other UI components).

Practical Examples:

15 practical examples of DHTML components that enhance the interactivity and functionality of web pages. These examples show how to implement common UI elements and effects like dropdown menus, image sliders, accordions, and more using DHTML.

1. Drop-down Menus:

A menu that appears when a user hovers over or clicks a menu item.

```
<ul>
  <li><a href="#">Menu</a>
    <ul>
      <li><a href="#">Submenu 1</a></li>
      <li><a href="#">Submenu 2</a></li>
    </ul>
  </li>
</ul>
<style>
  ul ul { display: none; }
  li:hover > ul { display: block; }
</style>
```

2. Image Sliders:

Automatically changing images in a slider with next and previous buttons.

```
let currentIndex = 0;
const images = document.querySelectorAll(".slider img");
function nextImage() {
  images[currentIndex].style.display = "none";
  currentIndex = (currentIndex + 1) % images.length;
  images[currentIndex].style.display = "block";
}
setInterval(nextImage, 3000); // Automatically change image every 3 seconds
```

3. Accordion:

A collapsible section that expands or collapses when clicked.

```html
<div class="accordion">
  <button class="accordion-button">Section 1</button>
  <div class="panel">
    <p>Content for section 1.</p>
  </div>
  <button class="accordion-button">Section 2</button>
  <div class="panel">
    <p>Content for section 2.</p>
  </div>
</div>

<script>
  const buttons = document.querySelectorAll('.accordion-button');
  buttons.forEach(button => {
    button.addEventListener('click', () => {
      const panel = button.nextElementSibling;
      panel.style.display = panel.style.display === 'block' ? 'none' :
'block';
    });
  });
</script>
```

4. Tab Navigation:

A simple tab system where content switches when a tab is clicked.

```html
<div class="tabs">
  <button class="tab-button">Tab 1</button>
  <button class="tab-button">Tab 2</button>
</div>
<div class="tab-content">
  <div>Tab 1 Content</div>
  <div>Tab 2 Content</div>
</div>

<script>
  const buttons = document.querySelectorAll('.tab-button');
  const contents = document.querySelectorAll('.tab-content div');
  buttons.forEach((button, index) => {
    button.addEventListener('click', () => {
      contents.forEach(content => content.style.display = 'none');
      contents[index].style.display = 'block';
    });
  });
</script>
```

5. Modal Window:

A popup modal that appears when a button is clicked.

```
<button id="openModal">Open Modal</button>
<div id="modal" style="display: none;">
  <div class="modal-content">
    <span id="closeModal">&times;</span>
    <p>Modal content here</p>
  </div>
</div>

<script>
  document.getElementById('openModal').addEventListener('click', () => {
    document.getElementById('modal').style.display = 'block';
  });
  document.getElementById('closeModal').addEventListener('click', () => {
    document.getElementById('modal').style.display = 'none';
  });
</script>
```

6. Tooltip:

A small pop-up box that appears when a user hovers over an element.

```
<button class="tooltip">Hover over me
  <span class="tooltip-text">Tooltip text</span>
</button>

<style>
  .tooltip .tooltip-text {
    display: none;
    position: absolute;
    background-color: black;
    color: white;
    padding: 5px;
    border-radius: 4px;
  }

  .tooltip:hover .tooltip-text {
    display: block;
  }
</style>
```

7. Image Gallery:

A gallery where images can be clicked to expand into a larger view.

```
<div class="gallery">
  <img src="image1.jpg" class="thumbnail" onclick="viewImage('image1.jpg')"
/>
  <img src="image2.jpg" class="thumbnail" onclick="viewImage('image2.jpg')"
/>
```

```
</div>

<div id="modalView" style="display: none;">
  <img id="modalImage" />
  <button onclick="closeModal()">Close</button>
</div>

<script>
  function viewImage(src) {
    document.getElementById('modalImage').src = src;
    document.getElementById('modalView').style.display = 'block';
  }

  function closeModal() {
    document.getElementById('modalView').style.display = 'none';
  }
</script>
```

8. Scroll to Top Button:

A button that appears when the user scrolls down and brings them back to the top of the page.

```
<button id="scrollToTop" onclick="scrollTop()">↑</button>

<script>
  window.onscroll = () => {
    document.getElementById('scrollToTop').style.display = window.scrollY >
200 ? 'block' : 'none';
  };

  function scrollTop() {
    window.scrollTo({ top: 0, behavior: 'smooth' });
  }
</script>
```

9. Collapsible Sidebar:

A sidebar that collapses or expands when clicked.

```
<div id="sidebar" style="width: 250px; background: #ddd;">
  <button onclick="toggleSidebar()">Toggle Sidebar</button>
</div>

<script>
  let isOpen = false;
  function toggleSidebar() {
    document.getElementById('sidebar').style.width = isOpen ? '0' : '250px';
    isOpen = !isOpen;
  }
</script>
```

10. Countdown Timer:

A countdown timer that updates every second.

```
<div id="countdown"></div>

<script>
  const targetDate = new Date("January 1, 2026").getTime();

  setInterval(() => {
    const now = new Date().getTime();
    const distance = targetDate - now;

    const days = Math.floor(distance / (1000 * 60 * 60 * 24));
    const hours = Math.floor((distance % (1000 * 60 * 60 * 24)) / (1000 * 60
* 60));
    const minutes = Math.floor((distance % (1000 * 60 * 60)) / (1000 * 60));
    const seconds = Math.floor((distance % (1000 * 60)) / 1000);

    document.getElementById("countdown").innerHTML = `${days}d ${hours}h
${minutes}m ${seconds}s`;

    if (distance < 0) {
      clearInterval(interval);
      document.getElementById("countdown").innerHTML = "EXPIRED";
    }
  }, 1000);
</script>
```

11. Form Validation:

A form that validates the user input in real-time.

```
<form id="myForm">
  <input type="text" id="email" placeholder="Email" />
  <span id="emailError" style="color: red; display: none;">Invalid
Email</span>
  <button type="submit">Submit</button>
</form>

<script>
  document.getElementById('email').addEventListener('input', function() {
    const email = this.value;
    document.getElementById('emailError').style.display =
/.+@.+\..+/.test(email) ? 'none' : 'block';
  });
</script>
```

12. Drag and Drop:

A draggable element that can be dropped into a target area.

```
<div id="dragItem" draggable="true" ondragstart="drag(event)">Drag Me</div>
```

```
<div id="dropArea" ondrop="drop(event)" ondragover="allowDrop(event)">Drop
Here</div>

<script>
  function allowDrop(ev) {
    ev.preventDefault();
  }

  function drag(ev) {
    ev.dataTransfer.setData("text", ev.target.id);
  }

  function drop(ev) {
    ev.preventDefault();
    const data = ev.dataTransfer.getData("text");
    const draggedItem = document.getElementById(data);
    ev.target.appendChild(draggedItem);
  }
</script>
```

13. Search Filter:

A live search filter that filters results as the user types.

```
<input type="text" id="search" placeholder="Search..." />
<ul id="results">
  <li>Apple</li>
  <li>Banana</li>
  <li>Cherry</li>
</ul>

<script>
  document.getElementById('search').addEventListener('input', function() {
    const query = this.value.toLowerCase();
    const items = document.querySelectorAll('#results li');
    items.forEach(item => {
      item.style.display = item.textContent.toLowerCase().includes(query) ?
'block' : 'none';
    });
  });
</script>
```

14. Countdown Timer with Animation:

A timer that counts down with a dynamic effect.

```
<div id="countdownTimer">10</div>

<script>
  let timeLeft = 10;
  const timer = document.getElementById('countdownTimer');

  const interval = setInterval(() => {
    timeLeft--;
```

```
    timer.innerText = timeLeft;
    timer.style.transform = `scale(${1 + timeLeft / 20})`;    // Animate as it
counts down
    if (timeLeft <= 0) {
      clearInterval(interval);
    }
  }, 1000);
</script>
```

15. Progress Bar:

A progress bar that fills up as a task progresses.

```
<progress id="progressBar" value="0" max="100"></progress>
<button onclick="startProgress()">Start Progress</button>

<script>
  function startProgress() {
    let progress = 0;
    const interval = setInterval(() => {
      progress += 10;
      document.getElementById('progressBar').value = progress;
      if (progress >= 100) {
        clearInterval(interval);
      }
    }, 500);
  }
</script>
```

In conclusion, DHTML is a powerful combination of technologies that can significantly enhance the interactivity and dynamism of web pages. By utilizing CSS, JavaScript, and the DOM, developers can create visually appealing and highly responsive websites that engage users through interactive elements, animations, and real-time updates.

30 multiple-choice questions (MCQs)

1. What is DHTML and Why It's Useful?

1. **What does DHTML stand for?**
   o A) Dynamic HTML
   o B) Direct HTML
   o C) Digital HTML
   o D) Dynamic HyperText Markup Language
   o **Answer:** A) Dynamic HTML
2. **Which of the following is NOT a part of DHTML?**
   o A) HTML
   o B) CSS
   o C) JavaScript
   o D) Flash

- o **Answer:** D) Flash
3. **Which of the following is a key advantage of DHTML?**
   - o A) Slower page load times
   - o B) Real-time interactivity
   - o C) Increased server load
   - o D) Less server interaction
   - o **Answer:** B) Real-time interactivity
4. **How does DHTML reduce server load?**
   - o A) By making requests for every user action
   - o B) By processing everything on the server
   - o C) By manipulating the content client-side
   - o D) By sending frequent requests to external APIs
   - o **Answer:** C) By manipulating the content client-side
5. **What is a primary benefit of using DHTML over static HTML?**
   - o A) Less code
   - o B) More dynamic and interactive web pages
   - o C) Faster load times
   - o D) Decreased interactivity
   - o **Answer:** B) More dynamic and interactive web pages

---

2. Adding Interactivity to Web Pages with DHTML

6. **Which JavaScript event can be used to detect a mouse click in DHTML?**
   - o A) onClick
   - o B) onLoad
   - o C) onSubmit
   - o D) onHover
   - o **Answer:** A) onClick
7. **What happens when you use JavaScript to modify the CSS properties of an element?**
   - o A) The page reloads
   - o B) The content of the page disappears
   - o C) The appearance of the element is changed dynamically
   - o D) The element is removed from the page
   - o **Answer:** C) The appearance of the element is changed dynamically
8. **What does the DOM allow you to do in the context of DHTML?**
   - o A) Only modify text content
   - o B) Access and manipulate HTML elements and CSS
   - o C) Load new pages dynamically
   - o D) Replace JavaScript entirely
   - o **Answer:** B) Access and manipulate HTML elements and CSS
9. **Which of the following is an example of adding interactivity with DHTML?**
   - o A) Static text on a page
   - o B) Dynamic color change when the user hovers over a button
   - o C) Pre-loaded content on the page

- o D) Static drop-down menus
- o **Answer:** B) Dynamic color change when the user hovers over a button

10. **Which of the following actions can be achieved using DHTML?**
    - o A) Only altering the page content server-side
    - o B) Only changing the structure of the page
    - o C) Changing the content, layout, and appearance dynamically based on user actions
    - o D) Static text formatting
    - o **Answer:** C) Changing the content, layout, and appearance dynamically based on user actions

3. Understanding CSS, JavaScript, and the DOM (Document Object Model)

11. **Which of these technologies is responsible for the visual styling of a webpage in DHTML?**
    - o A) HTML
    - o B) CSS
    - o C) JavaScript
    - o D) DOM
    - o **Answer:** B) CSS

12. **Which JavaScript function is used to access an HTML element by its ID?**
    - o A) getElementById()
    - o B) getElementByClass()
    - o C) querySelector()
    - o D) getElementByTagName()
    - o **Answer:** A) getElementById()

13. **The Document Object Model (DOM) represents the web page as a:**
    - o A) Single object
    - o B) Tree of nodes
    - o C) Flat list of elements
    - o D) File structure
    - o **Answer:** B) Tree of nodes

14. **What does CSS enable in the context of DHTML?**
    - o A) Changing page structure
    - o B) Adding JavaScript interactivity
    - o C) Defining the look and layout of page elements
    - o D) Creating dynamic content
    - o **Answer:** C) Defining the look and layout of page elements

15. **How can JavaScript interact with the DOM in DHTML?**
    - o A) It can only read data from the DOM
    - o B) It can only modify data on the server
    - o C) It can access and modify the DOM elements in real-time
    - o D) It cannot interact with the DOM
    - o **Answer:** C) It can access and modify the DOM elements in real-time

4. Manipulating Page Elements Using DHTML

16. **Which JavaScript method can be used to change the content of an element in DHTML?**
    - A) innerHTML
    - B) value
    - C) contentText
    - D) textContent
    - **Answer:** A) innerHTML

17. **To modify the background color of an element using JavaScript, which property should be used?**
    - A) style.color
    - B) style.background
    - C) style.backgroundColor
    - D) style.fontColor
    - **Answer:** C) style.backgroundColor

18. **Which JavaScript method can hide an HTML element by changing its display property?**
    - A) style.display = "none"
    - B) style.visibility = "hidden"
    - C) hideElement()
    - D) document.remove()
    - **Answer:** A) style.display = "none"

19. **What is the purpose of using the `style.position` property in DHTML?**
    - A) To change the content of an element
    - B) To set the size of an element
    - C) To modify the element's position on the page
    - D) To modify the font of an element
    - **Answer:** C) To modify the element's position on the page

20. **Which of the following is an example of manipulating page elements using DHTML?**
    - A) Adding a new element to the page dynamically
    - B) Altering an element's position using JavaScript
    - C) Changing an element's appearance in response to user input
    - D) All of the above
    - **Answer:** D) All of the above

---

5. Animation and Effects with DHTML

21. **Which of the following JavaScript methods can create a basic animation effect?**
    - A) setInterval()
    - B) setTimeout()
    - C) animate()
    - D) requestAnimationFrame()
    - **Answer:** D) requestAnimationFrame()

22. **Which CSS property is commonly used to animate the transition between two states (like colors or positions)?**
    - ○ A) transform
    - ○ B) transition
    - ○ C) animation
    - ○ D) keyframes
    - ○ **Answer:** B) transition
23. **What type of effect can be created using DHTML and JavaScript?**
    - ○ A) Smooth fade-in or fade-out
    - ○ B) Static page display
    - ○ C) Only text-based animations
    - ○ D) Automatic content population
    - ○ **Answer:** A) Smooth fade-in or fade-out
24. **What is the purpose of the `requestAnimationFrame()` method in DHTML animations?**
    - ○ A) To create a delay between animation frames
    - ○ B) To change the color of elements
    - ○ C) To optimize performance and create smooth animations
    - ○ D) To stop an animation immediately
    - ○ **Answer:** C) To optimize performance and create smooth animations
25. **Which of the following is an example of an animation effect in DHTML?**
    - ○ A) Fading an element in and out
    - ○ B) Changing an element's content
    - ○ C) Making a form submit automatically
    - ○ D) Displaying a static image on the page
    - ○ **Answer:** A) Fading an element in and out
26. **Which property is used to animate background color changes in CSS?**
    - ○ A) transition
    - ○ B) animation
    - ○ C) transform
    - ○ D) fade
    - ○ **Answer:** A) transition
27. **In DHTML, how can you simulate moving an element across the screen?**
    - ○ A) By changing the element's position with CSS and JavaScript
    - ○ B) By using HTML tags
    - ○ C) By adding additional HTML elements to the page
    - ○ D) By using a server-side language
    - ○ **Answer:** A) By changing the element's position with CSS and JavaScript
28. **Which of the following is a CSS property that can be animated for visual effects in DHTML?**
    - ○ A) color
    - ○ B) font-size
    - ○ C) opacity
    - ○ D) All of the above
    - ○ **Answer:** D) All of the above

29. **What is the primary advantage of using CSS transitions for animation over JavaScript-based methods?**
    - o A) JavaScript-based methods are faster
    - o B) CSS transitions are more efficient and require less code
    - o C) CSS cannot be used for animations
    - o D) JavaScript provides smoother effects
    - o **Answer:** B) CSS transitions are more efficient and require less code
30. **Which JavaScript function is typically used to create a smooth animation effect in DHTML?**
    - o A) setInterval()
    - o B) animate()
    - o C) setTimeout()
    - o D) querySelector()
    - o **Answer:** B) animate()

30 short questions and answers

1. What is DHTML and Why It's Useful?

1. **What is DHTML?**
    - o **Answer:** DHTML (Dynamic HTML) is a collection of web technologies (HTML, CSS, JavaScript, and DOM) used together to create interactive and dynamic web pages that can change content and appearance without reloading the page.
2. **Why is DHTML useful for web development?**
    - o **Answer:** DHTML enhances user experience by providing real-time interactivity, reducing server load, and enabling smooth animations and dynamic content updates without requiring page reloads.
3. **Which technologies are part of DHTML?**
    - o **Answer:** DHTML involves HTML, CSS, JavaScript, and the Document Object Model (DOM).
4. **How does DHTML improve web page interactivity?**
    - o **Answer:** DHTML allows web pages to respond to user actions like mouse clicks, hover events, and keyboard inputs, making the content more interactive and engaging.
5. **Does DHTML require server-side interaction?**
    - o **Answer:** No, DHTML primarily works client-side, reducing the need for frequent communication with the server for user interactions.

2. Adding Interactivity to Web Pages with DHTML

6. **How can DHTML add interactivity to a web page?**
    - o **Answer:** By using JavaScript to detect events (like clicks or hover) and modify the HTML or CSS dynamically based on those events.
7. **What type of interactivity can be achieved using DHTML?**
    - o **Answer:** Interactivities such as mouse events, real-time content updates, form validation, and element visibility changes.

8. **What is an example of a mouse event in DHTML?**
   - **Answer:** A mouse event can be a `click`, `mouseover`, or `mouseout` that triggers a specific action, such as showing or hiding an element.
9. **How does JavaScript handle user input in DHTML?**
   - **Answer:** JavaScript can capture user input from forms, validate it, and dynamically update the page content without refreshing.
10. **What happens when a user hovers over a button in DHTML?**
    - **Answer:** The button's appearance (e.g., color or size) can change dynamically through JavaScript or CSS, providing immediate visual feedback.

3. Understanding CSS, JavaScript, and the DOM (Document Object Model)

11. **What role does CSS play in DHTML?**
    - **Answer:** CSS controls the visual presentation and layout of HTML elements, and with DHTML, CSS can be dynamically changed using JavaScript.
12. **How does JavaScript work with DHTML?**
    - **Answer:** JavaScript is used to interact with HTML and CSS, allowing for dynamic changes to content, styles, and element positioning based on user actions.
13. **What is the DOM in the context of DHTML?**
    - **Answer:** The DOM (Document Object Model) is a tree-like structure that represents the HTML document. JavaScript can manipulate the DOM to change elements and their properties.
14. **How does JavaScript interact with the DOM?**
    - **Answer:** JavaScript accesses the DOM to retrieve and modify HTML elements, their content, and styles in real-time.
15. **Can CSS be modified dynamically with JavaScript in DHTML?**
    - **Answer:** Yes, JavaScript can modify CSS properties of elements on the page, such as changing background colors, sizes, or visibility.

4. Manipulating Page Elements Using DHTML

16. **How can you change the content of an HTML element using JavaScript?**
    - **Answer:** Use the `innerHTML` property to change the content of an element, such as `document.getElementById("elementId").innerHTML = "New Content";`.
17. **What JavaScript method is used to hide an element?**
    - **Answer:** Use the `style.display = "none"` property to hide an element.
18. **How can you change the background color of an element dynamically with JavaScript?**
    - **Answer:** Use `element.style.backgroundColor = "color";` to change an element's background color.
19. **What is the `style.position` property used for in DHTML?**
    - **Answer:** It allows you to change the positioning of an element on the page, such as `absolute`, `relative`, or `fixed`.

20. **How can you move an element across the page in DHTML?**
    - o **Answer:** You can change an element's `style.left` or `style.top` properties using JavaScript to position it dynamically.

5. Animation and Effects with DHTML

21. **What is the purpose of animations in DHTML?**
    - o **Answer:** Animations in DHTML enhance the user experience by smoothly transitioning between element states, such as fading in/out, sliding, or changing colors.
22. **How do CSS transitions work in DHTML?**
    - o **Answer:** CSS transitions allow smooth changes in CSS properties (like background color or position) when an element changes state, such as on hover.
23. **How can JavaScript create animations in DHTML?**
    - o **Answer:** JavaScript can update element properties over time, such as moving an element or changing its color gradually using `setInterval()`, `setTimeout()`, or `requestAnimationFrame()`.
24. **What is `requestAnimationFrame()` used for in DHTML?**
    - o **Answer:** It provides a way to create smooth, optimized animations by allowing the browser to control the timing of animation frames.
25. **What is an example of a fade-in effect using CSS?**
    - o **Answer:** Using `opacity` with CSS: `#element { opacity: 0; transition: opacity 1s; } #element:hover { opacity: 1; }`.
26. **How can you animate the movement of an element with JavaScript?**
    - o **Answer:** Use JavaScript to incrementally change the position of an element over time by updating its `style.left` or `style.top` properties.
27. **What is the difference between CSS animations and JavaScript animations?**
    - o **Answer:** CSS animations are easier to implement and use the `@keyframes` rule, while JavaScript animations offer more control but may require more code.
28. **What effect can be achieved with DHTML animations?**
    - o **Answer:** DHTML can create effects like sliding menus, fading elements in and out, or moving objects across the page.
29. **What is the benefit of using CSS transitions for animation over JavaScript?**
    - o **Answer:** CSS transitions are simpler to implement, more efficient, and less code-intensive for simple animations compared to JavaScript.
30. **Can you combine CSS and JavaScript for animations in DHTML?**
    - o **Answer:** Yes, CSS and JavaScript can be used together, where JavaScript handles event triggering and CSS manages the animation itself.

CHAPTER 4: INTRODUCTION TO JAVASCRIPT

What is JavaScript and How It Enhances Web Pages?

JavaScript is a high-level, interpreted programming language that is widely used to create interactive and dynamic web pages. Initially developed by Netscape, JavaScript has become an essential part of modern web development. It allows developers to add behavior and functionality to web pages, turning static HTML into interactive, real-time web applications.

Unlike HTML (Hypertext Markup Language) and CSS (Cascading Style Sheets), which focus on the structure and appearance of web pages, **JavaScript** brings these pages to life by enabling user interaction, content manipulation, and visual effects.

JavaScript runs in the user's **browser** (client-side), meaning that when a user interacts with a web page, JavaScript executes the corresponding actions without needing to refresh or reload the page. This enables fast response times and reduces the need for frequent server requests, improving overall performance.

In addition to client-side scripting, JavaScript can also run on the server side (through environments like **Node.js**), making it versatile and useful for both client-side and server-side development.

How JavaScript Enhances Web Pages:

1. Interactivity:

One of the primary ways JavaScript enhances web pages is by adding interactivity. It allows web pages to respond to user actions, such as mouse clicks, hovering, key presses, and form submissions. For example, when a user clicks a button, JavaScript can trigger specific actions, like showing or hiding an element, displaying a message, or even changing the content of a page.

- **Example:** A button click that triggers an alert or a change in text.

```
<button onclick="changeText()">Click me!</button>
<p id="text">Old text</p>

<script>
  function changeText() {
    document.getElementById("text").innerHTML = "New text";
  }
</script>
```

In this example, the text changes dynamically when the user clicks the button. JavaScript's ability to detect user input and respond accordingly is what makes a website feel interactive and responsive.

2. Dynamic Content:

JavaScript makes it possible to change the content of a webpage without having to reload it. You can modify the HTML, update CSS styles, and add or remove elements in response to user actions.

For instance, JavaScript can update a user's profile information in real-time or dynamically load new content without requiring the user to refresh the page.

- **Example:** Updating content in real-time without reloading the page.

```
<div id="message">Hello, User!</div>
<button onclick="updateMessage()">Update Message</button>

<script>
  function updateMessage() {
    document.getElementById("message").innerHTML = "Welcome back,
User!";
  }
</script>
```

In this example, the content inside the `<div>` is dynamically updated when the button is clicked, making the page feel more interactive and fluid.

3. Animations and Effects:

JavaScript is commonly used to create animations and visual effects, improving the user experience by providing smooth transitions between different states. This can include animations like fading in and out, sliding elements, resizing, or moving objects across the screen.

- **Example:** A simple fade effect with JavaScript.

```
<div id="box" style="width:100px;height:100px;background-
color:blue;"></div>
<button onclick="fadeOut()">Fade Out</button>

<script>
  function fadeOut() {
    var element = document.getElementById("box");
    var opacity = 1;
    var fadeEffect = setInterval(function() {
      if (opacity <= 0) {
        clearInterval(fadeEffect);
        element.style.display = "none";
      } else {
        opacity -= 0.1;
        element.style.opacity = opacity;
      }
    }, 50);
  }
</script>
```

In this example, clicking the button causes the blue box to fade out smoothly, demonstrating how JavaScript can be used to create fluid visual effects without requiring external libraries or complex code.

4. Asynchronous Operations:

JavaScript also supports asynchronous operations, meaning it can handle tasks like fetching data from a server in the background without blocking the rest of the page. This is particularly useful for web applications that need to request and display data dynamically.

For example, JavaScript can be used to send an AJAX (Asynchronous JavaScript and XML) request to a server to fetch new data (e.g., news articles or social media updates) and then update the content on the page without needing to refresh it.

- **Example:** Fetching data from an API without reloading the page (AJAX request).

```
var xhr = new XMLHttpRequest();
xhr.open("GET", "https://api.example.com/data", true);
xhr.onreadystatechange = function() {
  if (xhr.readyState == 4 && xhr.status == 200) {
    document.getElementById("content").innerHTML = xhr.responseText;
  }
};
xhr.send();
```

In this example, JavaScript fetches data from an API and dynamically updates the content of a webpage, providing a seamless user experience.

5. Form Validation:

JavaScript is widely used for **client-side form validation**, which ensures that the data entered by the user in a form is correct before it is submitted to the server. This reduces the number of invalid form submissions and improves the usability of the website.

For example, JavaScript can check that a user has entered a valid email address or that all required fields have been filled out.

- **Example:** Form validation for an email field.

```
<form onsubmit="return validateForm()">
  <label for="email">Email:</label>
  <input type="text" id="email" name="email">
  <input type="submit" value="Submit">
</form>

<script>
  function validateForm() {
    var email = document.getElementById("email").value;
    if (email === "" || !email.includes("@")) {
      alert("Please enter a valid email address.");
```

```
        return false; // Prevent form submission
      }
      return true;
    }
</script>
```

In this example, when the form is submitted, JavaScript checks if the email field is filled out and contains the "@" symbol. If not, it shows an alert and prevents the form submission.

6. Browser Control:

JavaScript can manipulate the **browser environment** itself, such as opening new windows, changing the URL, or modifying the history state without actually reloading the page. This feature is particularly useful in single-page applications (SPAs), where you want to change the content or navigation while keeping the page intact.

- **Example:** Changing the browser's URL without reloading the page.

```
window.history.pushState({}, "", "/new-page");
```

This command changes the browser's URL to "/new-page" without actually navigating to that URL or refreshing the page, which is useful in SPAs.

Basics of JavaScript Syntax: Variables, Functions, and Operators

JavaScript syntax is the set of rules that defines a correctly structured JavaScript program. To understand how JavaScript works, it's important to grasp the foundational concepts like variables, functions, and operators. Let's dive deeper into each of these concepts.

1. Variables in JavaScript

A **variable** in JavaScript is a named container used to store data, which can later be accessed or modified. JavaScript offers several ways to declare variables, each with its specific use cases and behavior.

Types of Variable Declarations:

- `let`: Used to declare variables that can be reassigned later. Variables declared with `let` are block-scoped, meaning they are accessible only within the block of code where they are defined.

  Example:

```
let x = 10; // Variable declared using 'let'
x = 20; // Reassigning value to 'x'
console.log(x); // Output: 20
```

- **const**: Used for variables that should never be reassigned after their initial value is set. const is also block-scoped like let.

    Example:

    ```
    const pi = 3.14; // Constant value cannot be reassigned
    console.log(pi); // Output: 3.14
    // pi = 3.14159; // This will result in an error because 'const' cannot
    be reassigned.
    ```

- **var**: This is the older way to declare variables. It is function-scoped, which can lead to unexpected behaviors when used in loops or conditional blocks. Due to its scoping issues, var is now less recommended in modern JavaScript.

    Example:

    ```
    var name = "John"; // Variable declared using 'var'
    console.log(name); // Output: John
    ```

2. Functions in JavaScript

A **function** is a block of reusable code designed to perform a specific task. Functions can take **parameters** (inputs) and return a **value** (output). They allow for modular and maintainable code.

Function Declaration:

The syntax for declaring a function starts with the function keyword, followed by the **function name**, a list of **parameters** in parentheses, and a block of code inside curly braces {}.

Example:

```
function greet(name) {
    return "Hello, " + name;
}

console.log(greet("Alice")); // Output: Hello, Alice
```

In this example, the function greet takes one parameter name, and returns a greeting string. When we call the function with the argument "Alice", it outputs "Hello, Alice".

Function with Multiple Parameters and Return Values:

A function can take multiple parameters and can return complex values like objects or arrays.

Example:

```
function add(a, b) {
    return a + b;  // Returning the sum of 'a' and 'b'
}

console.log(add(5, 3)); // Output: 8
```

In this example, the function `add` takes two parameters `a` and `b`, and returns their sum.

3. Operators in JavaScript

Operators in JavaScript are used to perform operations on variables and values. There are several categories of operators:

a. Arithmetic Operators:

These are used to perform basic mathematical operations.

- + (addition)
- − (subtraction)
- * (multiplication)
- / (division)
- % (modulus - returns the remainder of division)

Example:

```
let a = 5;
let b = 10;
let sum = a + b;  // Addition operator
console.log(sum);   // Output: 15

let remainder = b % a;  // Modulus operator
console.log(remainder);  // Output: 0
```

b. Comparison Operators:

These are used to compare two values and return a Boolean result (`true` or `false`).

- == (equal to)
- === (strictly equal to, also checks for type)
- != (not equal to)
- > (greater than)
- < (less than)
- >= (greater than or equal to)
- <= (less than or equal to)

Example:

```
let x = 5;
let y = 10;
let isEqual = (x === y); // Checks if x is strictly equal to y
console.log(isEqual);  // Output: false

let isGreaterThan = (y > x);  // Checks if y is greater than x
console.log(isGreaterThan);  // Output: true
```

c. Logical Operators:

These are used to combine multiple conditions and return a Boolean result.

- `&&` (logical AND)
- `||` (logical OR)
- `!` (logical NOT)

Example:

```
let x = 5;
let y = 10;
let isInRange = (x > 0 && y < 20); // Checks if x is greater than 0 AND y is
less than 20
console.log(isInRange);  // Output: true

let isFalse = !(x === 5); // Logical NOT operator
console.log(isFalse);  // Output: false
```

d. Assignment Operators:

These are used to assign values to variables, often with additional operations.

- `=` (assignment)
- `+=` (addition assignment)
- `-=` (subtraction assignment)
- `*=` (multiplication assignment)
- `/=` (division assignment)

Example:

```
let a = 5;
let b = 10;

a += b;  // Equivalent to: a = a + b
console.log(a);  // Output: 15

b *= 2;  // Equivalent to: b = b * 2
console.log(b);  // Output: 20
```

Event Handling: Responding to User Actions

Event handling in JavaScript allows developers to make web pages interactive by responding to user actions. These actions could be anything from a mouse click to a keyboard keypress, to more complex actions like form submissions or page loading. By using JavaScript's event handling features, you can create dynamic, user-driven interactions.

What Is Event Handling?

Event handling is the process of responding to specific actions or events that a user triggers on a webpage. For example, when a user clicks a button, the page can respond by showing a message, changing content, or executing a function. Event handling enables the creation of interactive web applications that react to user behavior without needing to reload the page.

JavaScript provides several ways to handle events, the most common being the `addEventListener()` method, which allows you to attach an event handler to an HTML element.

Basic Event Handling Example

Let's explore a simple example that demonstrates event handling. In this case, when a button is clicked, an alert is displayed.

```
<button id="myButton">Click Me!</button>

<script>
    // Select the button element by its ID
    document.getElementById("myButton").addEventListener("click", function()
{
        alert("Button was clicked!");
    });
</script>
```
Explanation:

1. **Selecting the Element**: We use the `getElementById()` method to select the button with the ID `"myButton"`. This allows us to target this specific button element on the page.
2. **Attaching the Event Listener**: The `addEventListener()` method is used to attach an event handler to the button. We specify that we want to listen for the `"click"` event on the button.
3. **The Event Handler**: When the button is clicked, the anonymous function we passed as the second argument to `addEventListener()` is executed. In this case, the function simply shows an alert saying `"Button was clicked!"`.

Flow of Execution:

- A user clicks the button.
- The `"click"` event is triggered.
- The event listener catches the event and runs the function that shows the alert.

This is a basic interaction in JavaScript, but it's foundational for building more complex interactive web applications.

Common Events in JavaScript

There are many types of events that JavaScript can listen for and respond to. Below are some of the most commonly used events:

1. `click` Event:

The `click` event occurs when a user clicks on an element, such as a button or a link.

Example:

```
document.getElementById("submitButton").addEventListener("click", function()
{
    alert("You clicked the submit button!");
});
```
2. `mouseover` Event:

The `mouseover` event occurs when the mouse pointer hovers over an element, such as a button, image, or text. This is useful for creating hover effects.

Example:

```
document.getElementById("hoverElement").addEventListener("mouseover",
function() {
    this.style.backgroundColor = "yellow"; // Changes the background color
when hovered
});
```
3. `keydown` Event:

The `keydown` event is triggered when a user presses a key on the keyboard. This can be used for form validation, capturing user input, or even for creating games.

Example:

```
document.addEventListener("keydown", function(event) {
    alert("You pressed the key: " + event.key); // Shows the key that was
pressed
```

```
});
```

4. submit Event:

The `submit` event occurs when a form is submitted, typically triggered by clicking a submit button or pressing `Enter` within an input field. It is commonly used for form validation before submitting the data to the server.

Example:

```
document.getElementById("myForm").addEventListener("submit", function(event)
{
    event.preventDefault();  // Prevents the default form submission
    alert("Form submitted!");
});
```

In this example, the `preventDefault()` method is used to stop the form from being submitted, which can be useful when performing client-side validation before allowing the form to submit.

5. load Event:

The `load` event occurs when the entire webpage (including all images, scripts, etc.) has finished loading. It's useful for initializing JavaScript functions or animations after the page is fully loaded.

Example:

```
window.addEventListener("load", function() {
    alert("Page has loaded completely!");
});
```

Event Propagation: Bubbling and Capturing

In JavaScript, events don't just affect the target element; they can "propagate" through the DOM tree. There are two phases of event propagation: **bubbling** and **capturing**.

1. **Bubbling**: When an event occurs on an element, it first triggers the event handler on the target element and then "bubbles up" to the parent elements.

   Example:

   ```
   document.getElementById("parentDiv").addEventListener("click",
   function() {
       alert("Parent div clicked!");
   });

   document.getElementById("childDiv").addEventListener("click",
   function() {
       alert("Child div clicked!");
   ```

```
});
```

If you click on `childDiv`, the alert for `"Child div clicked!"` will show first, followed by `"Parent div clicked!"`.

2. **Capturing**: The event starts from the top of the DOM tree and propagates down to the target element. It can be enabled by setting the third argument of `addEventListener()` to `true`.

Example:

```javascript
javascript
Copy code
document.getElementById("parentDiv").addEventListener("click",
function() {
    alert("Parent div clicked!");
}, true);   // Capturing phase
```

Removing Event Listeners

You can remove event listeners that were previously attached using `removeEventListener()`.

Example:

```
function alertMessage() {
    alert("This is an alert!");
}

document.getElementById("alertButton").addEventListener("click",
alertMessage);

// Remove the event listener after some condition
document.getElementById("removeButton").addEventListener("click", function()
{
    document.getElementById("alertButton").removeEventListener("click",
alertMessage);
    alert("Event listener removed!");
});
```

-

Working with DOM in JavaScript

The **DOM (Document Object Model)** is a programming interface that allows scripts (like JavaScript) to interact with and manipulate the structure, content, and style of HTML and XML documents. It represents the page as a tree structure, where each element is a node that can be accessed and modified. In the context of web development, the DOM allows developers to create dynamic, interactive web pages by enabling JavaScript to read and change the content and appearance of HTML elements.

JavaScript interacts with the DOM through various methods and properties, making it a powerful tool for building responsive web applications. The DOM enables the manipulation of HTML content, adding and removing elements, and changing their styles in real time without requiring a page reload.

Basic DOM Manipulation Example

Let's start with a simple example to demonstrate how JavaScript interacts with the DOM:

```
<p id="demo">This is a paragraph.</p>
<button onclick="changeText()">Click to Change Text</button>

<script>
    function changeText() {
        document.getElementById("demo").innerHTML = "Text has been changed!";
    }
</script>
```
Explanation:

1. **HTML Structure**: We have a paragraph (`<p>`) with the ID `"demo"` and a button that, when clicked, triggers the `changeText()` function.
2. **JavaScript Function**:
   o `document.getElementById("demo")`: This method is used to select the paragraph element by its `id` ("demo").
   o `.innerHTML = "Text has been changed!"`: This property is used to modify the content inside the selected element. In this case, we change the text of the paragraph when the button is clicked.
3. **Result**: When the user clicks the button, the content of the paragraph changes to `"Text has been changed!"`.

This is a basic example of how you can manipulate the DOM to update content dynamically without needing to reload the page.

Common DOM Methods

JavaScript provides several useful methods to interact with the DOM. Below are some of the most commonly used ones:

1. getElementById():

- **Purpose**: Selects an element by its `id` attribute.
- **Syntax**: `document.getElementById("id")`
- **Example**:

```
var element = document.getElementById("demo");
element.innerHTML = "New content";
```

2. getElementsByClassName():

- **Purpose**: Selects all elements with a specific class name.
- **Syntax**: `document.getElementsByClassName("className")`
- **Example**:

```
var elements = document.getElementsByClassName("myClass");
elements[0].style.color = "blue"; // Changes the text color of the
first element with 'myClass'
```

This method returns a collection of elements (not just one), so you would need to reference individual elements by their index in the returned collection.

3. querySelector():

- **Purpose**: Selects the first element that matches a specified CSS selector.
- **Syntax**: `document.querySelector("selector")`
- **Example**:

```
javascript
Copy code
var firstButton = document.querySelector(".myButton");
firstButton.style.backgroundColor = "yellow";
```

This method allows more flexible selection, such as selecting elements by class, ID, attribute, etc.

4. createElement():

- **Purpose**: Creates a new HTML element.
- **Syntax**: `document.createElement("tagName")`
- **Example**:

```
var newDiv = document.createElement("div");
newDiv.innerHTML = "This is a new div!";
document.body.appendChild(newDiv); // Appends the new div to the body
```

This method does not automatically add the created element to the page; it creates the element in memory. You must then append it to the DOM using methods like `appendChild()` or `insertBefore()`.

5. appendChild():

- **Purpose**: Adds a new child node (element) to a specified parent node.
- **Syntax**: `parentNode.appendChild(childNode)`
- **Example**:

```
var newPara = document.createElement("p");
newPara.textContent = "This is a new paragraph!";
document.getElementById("content").appendChild(newPara);   // Appends
the new paragraph to the element with ID 'content'
```

This method adds the created element to the DOM and makes it visible on the webpage.

6. removeChild():

- **Purpose**: Removes a child node from a parent node.
- **Syntax**: `parentNode.removeChild(childNode)`
- **Example**:

```
var parentElement = document.getElementById("content");
var childElement = document.getElementById("toRemove");
parentElement.removeChild(childElement);   // Removes the 'toRemove'
element from 'content'
```

7. setAttribute():

- **Purpose**: Sets an attribute of an element to a specified value.
- **Syntax**: `element.setAttribute("attribute", "value")`
- **Example**:

```
var img = document.getElementById("myImage");
img.setAttribute("src", "newImage.jpg");   // Changes the image source
to 'newImage.jpg'
```

8. getAttribute():

- **Purpose**: Retrieves the value of an attribute of an element.
- **Syntax**: `element.getAttribute("attribute")`
- **Example**:

```
var img = document.getElementById("myImage");
var source = img.getAttribute("src");   // Retrieves the 'src' attribute
of the image
```

Manipulating Styles in the DOM

In addition to modifying content, you can also change the CSS styles of elements dynamically. This is done through the `style` property of DOM elements:

```
document.getElementById("myDiv").style.color = "red"; // Changes the text
color to red
document.getElementById("myDiv").style.backgroundColor = "yellow"; // Changes
the background color
document.getElementById("myDiv").style.fontSize = "20px"; // Changes the font
size to 20px
```

The `style` property allows you to manipulate inline styles, but for complex style changes, it's often better to manipulate classes or use `classList` methods.

Creating and Manipulating Lists of Elements

You can select multiple elements and iterate over them, especially when working with collections of elements returned by methods like `getElementsByClassName()` or `querySelectorAll()`:

```
var allParagraphs = document.querySelectorAll("p");
allParagraphs.forEach(function(paragraph) {
    paragraph.style.color = "green";  // Changes the color of all paragraphs
});
```

Validating Forms with JavaScript

Form validation is an essential part of web development to ensure that the data submitted by users meets the required criteria before it reaches the server. JavaScript allows developers to perform client-side form validation, which can greatly enhance user experience by providing immediate feedback. By validating forms before submission, you can ensure that the data is accurate and that the user has entered it in the correct format.

JavaScript form validation can check for a variety of conditions such as:

- **Required Fields**: Ensuring the user has filled out necessary fields.
- **Email Format**: Validating that the email entered has a proper format (e.g., contains "@" and domain).
- **Password Strength**: Checking that the password meets specific security criteria, such as length and character variety.
- **Numeric Input**: Ensuring only numeric values are entered where appropriate.

Example of Simple Form Validation

Let's look at an example where we validate an email field in a form. The form ensures that the email entered by the user contains the "@" symbol, which is a basic check for valid email format.

```
<form id="myForm">
```

```
    <label for="email">Email:</label>
    <input type="email" id="email" name="email" required>
    <input type="submit" value="Submit">
</form>

<script>
    document.getElementById("myForm").onsubmit = function(event) {
        const email = document.getElementById("email").value;
        // Check if the email contains "@"
        if (!email.includes("@")) {
            alert("Please enter a valid email address.");
            event.preventDefault(); // Prevent form submission if the
validation fails
        }
    }
</script>
```
Explanation:

1. **HTML Form**:
    o The form contains a single email input field (`<input type="email">`) and a submit button.
    o The `required` attribute in the email input ensures that the field cannot be left empty.
2. **JavaScript Validation**:
    o The `onsubmit` event is triggered when the form is submitted.
    o The function retrieves the value entered in the email field using `document.getElementById("email").value`.
    o It checks if the email contains the "@" symbol using `email.includes("@")`. If it does not, an alert is shown and the form submission is prevented using `event.preventDefault()`. This stops the form from being submitted until the user corrects the input.
3. **Result**:
    o If the email is valid (contains "@"), the form is submitted as normal.
    o If the email is invalid (doesn't contain "@"), an alert is shown, and the form submission is blocked.

Common Validation Techniques

JavaScript can be used to validate a wide variety of conditions in a form. Below are some common validation techniques and examples:

1. Required Fields

To check if a field has been filled out, we can use the `required` attribute in HTML, but JavaScript can also check for missing required fields programmatically.

Example:

```
document.getElementById("myForm").onsubmit = function(event) {
    const name = document.getElementById("name").value;
    if (name === "") {
        alert("Name field is required.");
        event.preventDefault(); // Prevent submission if field is empty
    }
}
```

2. Email Format Validation

A more advanced email validation involves checking if the email entered matches a proper email format. You can use a regular expression (regex) for this.

Example:

```
document.getElementById("myForm").onsubmit = function(event) {
    const email = document.getElementById("email").value;
    const emailPattern = /^[a-zA-Z0-9._-]+@[a-zA-Z0-9.-]+\.[a-zA-Z]{2,6}$/;
    if (!emailPattern.test(email)) {
        alert("Please enter a valid email address.");
        event.preventDefault(); // Prevent form submission
    }
}
```

This regex checks for:

- A series of characters followed by an "@" symbol.
- A domain name (with a dot in between).
- A valid domain extension (like .com, .org, etc.).

3. Password Strength Validation

For password fields, it's important to check that the password meets specific strength requirements (e.g., a minimum length, special characters, numbers).

Example:

```
document.getElementById("myForm").onsubmit = function(event) {
    const password = document.getElementById("password").value;
    const passwordPattern = /^(?=.*\d)(?=.*[a-z])(?=.*[A-Z]).{6,20}$/;
    if (!passwordPattern.test(password)) {
        alert("Password must be between 6 to 20 characters long and include
at least one uppercase letter, one lowercase letter, and one digit.");
        event.preventDefault(); // Prevent form submission
    }
}
```

This regular expression checks for:

- A password length between 6 to 20 characters.
- At least one lowercase letter, one uppercase letter, and one number.

4. Numeric Input Validation

If you want to ensure that the user enters only numbers (for fields like age or quantity), you can validate the input.

Example:

```
document.getElementById("myForm").onsubmit = function(event) {
    const age = document.getElementById("age").value;
    if (isNaN(age) || age < 0) {
        alert("Please enter a valid positive number for age.");
        event.preventDefault(); // Prevent form submission
    }
}
```

The `isNaN()` function checks if the input is not a number, and we can also check if the value is greater than 0 to ensure it's a valid positive number.

5. Checkbox Validation

If a form requires the user to check a box (such as agreeing to terms and conditions), JavaScript can check whether the checkbox is checked.

Example:

```
document.getElementById("myForm").onsubmit = function(event) {
    const termsCheckbox = document.getElementById("terms");
    if (!termsCheckbox.checked) {
        alert("You must agree to the terms and conditions.");
        event.preventDefault(); // Prevent form submission
    }
}
```

Form Validation Best Practices

1. **Provide Clear Feedback**:
   - Use inline error messages or tooltips to show users where their input is incorrect.
   - Avoid using `alert()` for errors as it can be intrusive. Instead, display error messages directly on the form.
2. **Combine Client-Side and Server-Side Validation**:
   - Client-side validation can catch simple mistakes, but server-side validation is necessary for security and data integrity.

3. **Use HTML5 Built-in Validation**:
   o HTML5 provides some basic validation attributes like `required`, `pattern`, and `type="email"`. Combine these with JavaScript for more robust validation.

Practical Examples: Interactive Forms, Pop-up Alerts, and Simple Calculators

15 practical examples that show how JavaScript can enhance user interaction and functionality on web pages:

1. Dynamic Content Based on User Input

Example: Change the background color of a box based on the selected color from a dropdown.

```html
<select id="colorPicker">
    <option value="red">Red</option>
    <option value="green">Green</option>
    <option value="blue">Blue</option>
</select>
<div id="colorBox" style="width:100px; height:100px;"></div>

<script>
    document.getElementById("colorPicker").addEventListener("change",
function() {
        const selectedColor = this.value;
        document.getElementById("colorBox").style.backgroundColor =
selectedColor;
    });
</script>
```

Description: This example demonstrates how JavaScript dynamically updates the background color of a div based on user selection.

2. Pop-up Alerts

Example: Display a pop-up alert when a button is clicked.

```html
<button onclick="showAlert()">Click Me</button>

<script>
    function showAlert() {
        alert("This is a pop-up alert!");
    }
</script>
```

Description: A button triggers an alert message when clicked.

3. Simple Calculator

Example: Create a basic calculator to add two numbers entered by the user.

```
<input type="number" id="num1" placeholder="Enter a number">
<input type="number" id="num2" placeholder="Enter another number">
<button onclick="addNumbers()">Add</button>
<p id="result"></p>

<script>
    function addNumbers() {
        const num1 = parseInt(document.getElementById("num1").value);
        const num2 = parseInt(document.getElementById("num2").value);
        const result = num1 + num2;
        document.getElementById("result").innerText = "Result: " + result;
    }
</script>
```

Description: Adds two numbers and shows the result below the input fields.

4. Image Gallery with Lightbox Effect

Example: Click on an image to open it in a larger view with a lightbox effect.

```
<div class="gallery">
    <img src="image1.jpg" onclick="openLightbox('image1.jpg')">
    <img src="image2.jpg" onclick="openLightbox('image2.jpg')">
</div>

<div id="lightbox" style="display:none;">
    <img id="lightboxImage" src="" style="width:100%;">
    <button onclick="closeLightbox()">Close</button>
</div>

<script>
    function openLightbox(image) {
        document.getElementById("lightboxImage").src = image;
        document.getElementById("lightbox").style.display = "block";
    }
    function closeLightbox() {
        document.getElementById("lightbox").style.display = "none";
    }
</script>
```

Description: Clicking on any image opens it in a larger view with a close button to exit the lightbox.

5. Toggle Visibility of an Element

Example: Show or hide content when a button is clicked.

```
<button onclick="toggleVisibility()">Show/Hide Content</button>
```

```
<div id="content" style="display:none;">This is the content.</div>

<script>
    function toggleVisibility() {
        const content = document.getElementById("content");
        content.style.display = content.style.display === "none" ? "block" :
"none";
    }
</script>
```

Description: Toggles visibility of a div between "show" and "hide."

6. Countdown Timer

Example: Create a countdown timer that updates every second.

```
<p id="timer">10</p>

<script>
    let timeLeft = 10;
    setInterval(function() {
        document.getElementById("timer").innerText = timeLeft;
        timeLeft--;
        if (timeLeft < 0) {
            clearInterval();
            alert("Time's up!");
        }
    }, 1000);
</script>
```

Description: This countdown timer decreases by 1 every second and alerts the user when the time runs out.

7. Interactive Image Slider

Example: Create an image slider that automatically changes images.

```
<div class="slider">
    <img src="image1.jpg" class="slide" style="display:block;">
    <img src="image2.jpg" class="slide" style="display:none;">
    <img src="image3.jpg" class="slide" style="display:none;">
</div>

<script>
    let currentIndex = 0;
    const slides = document.querySelectorAll(".slide");

    function showNextSlide() {
        slides[currentIndex].style.display = "none";
        currentIndex = (currentIndex + 1) % slides.length;
        slides[currentIndex].style.display = "block";
    }
```

```
    setInterval(showNextSlide, 3000); // Changes slide every 3 seconds
</script>
```

Description: Automatically cycles through images in a slideshow every 3 seconds.

8. Real-time Character Count for a Textarea

Example: Display the remaining characters the user can type in a textarea.

```
<textarea id="text" maxlength="100"></textarea>
<p id="charCount">100 characters remaining</p>

<script>
    document.getElementById("text").addEventListener("input", function() {
        const remaining = 100 - this.value.length;
        document.getElementById("charCount").innerText = remaining + "
characters remaining";
    });
</script>
```

Description: Updates the character count dynamically as the user types.

9. Form Validation Before Submission

Example: Validate user input before form submission.

```
<form id="myForm">
    <input type="text" id="username" placeholder="Username">
    <input type="submit" value="Submit">
</form>

<script>
    document.getElementById("myForm").onsubmit = function(event) {
        const username = document.getElementById("username").value;
        if (!username) {
            alert("Username is required.");
            event.preventDefault(); // Prevent form submission
        }
    }
</script>
```

Description: Prevents form submission if the username field is empty.

10. Change Text Color

Example: Change the text color based on user selection.

```
<select id="colorPicker">
    <option value="red">Red</option>
    <option value="green">Green</option>
    <option value="blue">Blue</option>
```

```
</select>
<p id="text">Change my color!</p>

<script>
    document.getElementById("colorPicker").addEventListener("change",
function() {
        document.getElementById("text").style.color = this.value;
    });
</script>
```

Description: Change the text color of a paragraph based on the selected dropdown option.

11. Show Current Date and Time

Example: Display the current date and time.

```
<p id="currentDate"></p>

<script>
    function updateTime() {
        const now = new Date();
        document.getElementById("currentDate").innerText = now.toString();
    }

    setInterval(updateTime, 1000); // Update every second
</script>
```

Description: Shows the current date and time, updating every second.

12. Searchable Dropdown

Example: Create a searchable dropdown where the user can filter options as they type.

```
<input type="text" id="search" placeholder="Search...">
<ul id="dropdown">
    <li>Apple</li>
    <li>Banana</li>
    <li>Orange</li>
    <li>Peach</li>
</ul>

<script>
    document.getElementById("search").addEventListener("input", function() {
        const query = this.value.toLowerCase();
        const items = document.querySelectorAll("#dropdown li");
        items.forEach(item => {
            if (item.textContent.toLowerCase().includes(query)) {
                item.style.display = "block";
            } else {
                item.style.display = "none";
            }
        });
    });
```

```
</script>
```

Description: Filters the dropdown items based on the text entered in the input field.

13. Interactive Tooltip

Example: Show a tooltip when the user hovers over a button.

```
<button id="myButton">Hover me!</button>
<div id="tooltip" style="display:none; background-color:gray; color:white;
padding:5px; position:absolute;">This is a tooltip!</div>

<script>
    document.getElementById("myButton").addEventListener("mouseover",
function() {
        document.getElementById("tooltip").style.display = "block";
    });
    document.getElementById("myButton").addEventListener("mouseout",
function() {
        document.getElementById("tooltip").style.display = "none";
    });
</script>
```

Description: A tooltip appears when the user hovers over the button.

14. Toggle Dark/Light Mode

Example: Switch between dark and light modes for a webpage.

```
<button id="modeToggle">Toggle Dark/Light Mode</button>

<script>
    document.getElementById("modeToggle").addEventListener("click",
function() {
        document.body.classList.toggle("dark-mode");
    });
</script>

<style>
    body.dark-mode {
        background-color: black;
        color: white;
    }
</style>
```

Description: A button that switches the webpage between dark and light themes.

15. Password Strength Checker

Example: Check if a password meets certain strength criteria.

```
<input type="password" id="password" placeholder="Enter password">
<p id="strength"></p>

<script>
    document.getElementById("password").addEventListener("input", function()
{
        const password = this.value;
        const strengthMessage = document.getElementById("strength");
        if (password.length < 6) {
            strengthMessage.innerText = "Weak";
            strengthMessage.style.color = "red";
        } else if (password.length < 12) {
            strengthMessage.innerText = "Medium";
            strengthMessage.style.color = "orange";
        } else {
            strengthMessage.innerText = "Strong";
            strengthMessage.style.color = "green";
        }
    });
</script>
```

Description: Provides real-time feedback on password strength based on its length

---

Conclusion

JavaScript is essential for creating interactive, dynamic web pages. By mastering basic syntax (variables, functions, operators), understanding event handling, and using the DOM, you can enhance web pages with functionality like form validation, pop-up alerts, and interactive elements. With its ability to manipulate content, style, and behavior, JavaScript remains a crucial tool for modern web development.

30 multiple-choice questions (MCQs) covering the topics of JavaScript basics, event handling, DOM manipulation, and form validation:

1. What is JavaScript?

A) A markup language
B) A stylesheet language
C) A programming language
D) A server-side language

Answer: C) A programming language

2. Which of the following is NOT a characteristic of JavaScript?

A) It runs in the browser
B) It is a client-side language

C) It is used for creating static web pages
D) It can handle user interactions

Answer: C) It is used for creating static web pages

3. Which keyword is used to declare a variable in JavaScript that cannot be reassigned?

A) let
B) const
C) var
D) function

Answer: B) const

4. What does the 'let' keyword do in JavaScript?

A) It creates a constant variable
B) It creates a globally scoped variable
C) It creates a variable that can be reassigned
D) It defines a function

Answer: C) It creates a variable that can be reassigned

5. Which operator is used to add two numbers in JavaScript?

A) +
B) *
C) -
D) /

Answer: A) +

6. How do you create a function in JavaScript?

A) function myFunction() {}
B) create function myFunction() {}
C) def myFunction() {}
D) func myFunction() {}

Answer: A) function myFunction() {}

7. What is the correct syntax for an if statement in JavaScript?

A) if (x == 10) { }
B) if x == 10 { }
C) if x = 10 {}
D) if (x == 10); { }

Answer: A) if (x == 10) { }

8. Which of the following is a correct way to write a comment in JavaScript?

A) // This is a comment
B) /* This is a comment */
C) <!-- This is a comment -->
D) Both A and B

Answer: D) Both A and B

9. Which operator is used to compare both the value and type of two variables?

A) ==
B) ===
C) !=
D) =

Answer: B) ===

10. What is the purpose of the addEventListener method in JavaScript?

A) It adds an HTML element to the document
B) It listens for an event and executes a callback function
C) It removes an event listener
D) It creates a new event

Answer: B) It listens for an event and executes a callback function

11. Which of the following is an event in JavaScript?

A) click
B) load
C) submit
D) All of the above

Answer: D) All of the above

12. How do you add a click event listener to a button with id 'myButton' in JavaScript?

A) document.getElementById('myButton').addEventListener('click', function() {});
B) addEventListener('click', myButton);
C) document.getElementById('myButton').onclick = function() {};
D) All of the above

Answer: A) document.getElementById('myButton').addEventListener('click', function() {});

13. Which method is used to get the first element that matches a CSS selector in JavaScript?

A) getElementById()
B) getElementsByClassName()
C) querySelector()
D) querySelectorAll()

Answer: C) querySelector()

14. Which of the following methods can be used to access an element by its id in JavaScript?

A) getElementById()
B) getElementsByClassName()
C) querySelectorAll()
D) All of the above

Answer: A) getElementById()

15. Which of these methods creates a new HTML element in JavaScript?

A) createElement()
B) createNode()
C) addElement()
D) appendChild()

Answer: A) createElement()

16. Which of the following methods adds a new element to a parent element in the DOM?

A) appendChild()
B) insertBefore()

C) insertAfter()
D) removeChild()

Answer: A) appendChild()

17. Which JavaScript property is used to set or get the value of an input element?

A) innerHTML
B) value
C) textContent
D) content

Answer: B) value

18. What does the preventDefault() method do in event handling?

A) It stops the propagation of an event
B) It prevents the browser's default behavior
C) It cancels the event
D) Both A and B

Answer: D) Both A and B

19. Which JavaScript method is used to validate a form before submission?

A) validate()
B) checkValidity()
C) formValidation()
D) isValid()

Answer: B) checkValidity()

20. How can you prevent a form from being submitted in JavaScript?

A) Using event.preventDefault()
B) Using return false;
C) Using form.submit()
D) Both A and B

Answer: D) Both A and B

21. How do you check if a form input is empty using JavaScript?

A) if (input === "")
B) if (input == "")

C) if (input.value === "")
D) Both B and C

Answer: D) Both B and C

22. Which of these is NOT a valid JavaScript data type?

A) Number
B) String
C) Function
D) Character

Answer: D) Character

23. How can you access the text content of an element using JavaScript?

A) innerHTML
B) textContent
C) getText()
D) Both A and B

Answer: D) Both A and B

24. Which JavaScript method is used to delete an element from the DOM?

A) deleteChild()
B) remove()
C) destroy()
D) deleteElement()

Answer: B) remove()

25. Which JavaScript method allows you to change the style of an element dynamically?

A) getStyle()
B) setStyle()
C) style.set()
D) element.style.property

Answer: D) element.style.property

26. What is the purpose of using JavaScript to validate forms?

A) To make sure the user input is correct
B) To submit the form without server interaction
C) To display a form dynamically
D) To submit the form asynchronously

Answer: A) To make sure the user input is correct

27. Which function is used to show an alert box in JavaScript?

A) alert()
B) prompt()
C) confirm()
D) log()

Answer: A) alert()

28. Which JavaScript method is used to focus on an input element?

A) focus()
B) select()
C) input()
D) highlight()

Answer: A) focus()

29. Which JavaScript function is used to display a confirm dialog box?

A) prompt()
B) confirm()
C) alert()
D) dialog()

Answer: B) confirm()

30. Which attribute is used to get the value of an HTML element like an input or textarea in JavaScript?

A) textContent
B) innerHTML
C) value
D) content

Answer: C) value

30 short questions and answers covering various aspects of JavaScript basics, event handling, DOM manipulation, and form validation:

---

1. What is a variable in JavaScript?

- **Answer**: A variable is a container used to store data values. In JavaScript, you can declare variables using `let`, `const`, or `var`.

2. What is the difference between `let` and `const` in JavaScript?

- **Answer**: `let` allows reassignment of the variable, while `const` defines a constant value that cannot be reassigned.

3. How do you declare a function in JavaScript?

- **Answer**: A function is declared using the `function` keyword, followed by the function name and parentheses, e.g., `function myFunction() { }`.

4. What is the purpose of the `return` keyword in JavaScript?

- **Answer**: The `return` keyword is used to send a value from a function back to the caller.

5. What does the + operator do in JavaScript?

- **Answer**: The + operator performs addition if used with numbers or concatenation if used with strings.

6. What is an event in JavaScript?

- **Answer**: An event is an action that occurs in the browser, such as a click, hover, or keypress.

7. How do you add an event listener in JavaScript?

- **Answer**: You can add an event listener using `element.addEventListener('event', function)`, where `event` is the event type (like 'click') and `function` is the callback function.

8. What is the difference between `click` and `dblclick` events in JavaScript?

- **Answer**: `click` triggers when an element is clicked once, while `dblclick` triggers when the element is clicked twice in quick succession.

9. How can you prevent the default behavior of an event in JavaScript?

- **Answer**: Use `event.preventDefault()` to prevent the default behavior, such as stopping form submission or link navigation.

10. What is the `this` keyword in JavaScript?

- **Answer**: The `this` keyword refers to the current object or element that the function or method is being executed on.

11. How do you access an HTML element by its ID in JavaScript?

- **Answer**: You can use `document.getElementById('id')` to access an element by its ID.

12. What method would you use to select multiple elements with the same class name?

- **Answer**: Use `document.getElementsByClassName('className')` to select multiple elements by class name.

13. What is the purpose of `querySelector()` in JavaScript?

- **Answer**: `querySelector()` returns the first element that matches the specified CSS selector.

14. What is the role of the `innerHTML` property?

- **Answer**: `innerHTML` allows you to get or set the HTML content of an element.

15. How do you create a new HTML element in JavaScript?

- **Answer**: Use `document.createElement('element')` to create a new HTML element.

16. How do you append a new element to an existing parent element in JavaScript?

- **Answer**: Use `parentElement.appendChild(newElement)` to append a new element as a child.

17. How do you change the text content of an element in JavaScript?

- **Answer**: Use `element.textContent = 'new text'` to change the text content.

18. What is the `value` property used for in form elements?

- **Answer**: The `value` property is used to get or set the current value of form elements like input fields and text areas.

19. What is form validation in JavaScript?

- **Answer**: Form validation ensures that the user input is in the correct format before the form is submitted.

20. How can you check if an input field is empty in JavaScript?

- **Answer**: Use `if (input.value === '')` to check if an input field is empty.

21. How do you check if a user has entered a valid email address using JavaScript?

- **Answer**: You can use a regular expression (RegEx) to check for a valid email format, e.g., `/.+@.+\..+/`.

22. What is the `onsubmit` event used for in JavaScript?

- **Answer**: The `onsubmit` event is triggered when a form is submitted, and it can be used for form validation.

23. How do you stop a form from being submitted if validation fails?

- **Answer**: Use `event.preventDefault()` in the form's `onsubmit` handler to stop the submission.

24. How do you make sure a password meets a minimum length requirement in JavaScript?

- **Answer**: Use an `if` statement to check if `password.length >= 8` (or whatever length is required).

25. What is the `querySelectorAll()` method used for?

- **Answer**: `querySelectorAll()` selects all elements that match a CSS selector and returns them as a NodeList.

26. How do you remove an HTML element from the DOM in JavaScript?

- **Answer**: Use `element.remove()` to remove an element from the DOM.

27. How do you trigger an event manually in JavaScript?

- **Answer**: Use `element.dispatchEvent(new Event('eventName'))` to manually trigger an event.

28. How do you check the validity of a form field in JavaScript?

- **Answer**: You can use the `checkValidity()` method on a form field, e.g., `input.checkValidity()`.

29. How do you reset a form in JavaScript?

- **Answer**: Use `form.reset()` to reset all form fields to their default values.

30. How do you dynamically change the style of an element in JavaScript?

- **Answer**: Use `element.style.property = 'value'` to change the CSS style of an element, e.g., `element.style.backgroundColor = 'red'`.

CHAPTER 5: ADVANCED JAVASCRIPT CONCEPTS

1. Arrays, Loops, and Conditionals in JavaScript

Arrays are one of the fundamental data structures in JavaScript. An array allows you to store multiple values in a single variable, which makes managing related data much easier. Arrays in JavaScript are ordered collections, meaning that each element is indexed, starting from 0.

Declaring Arrays:

In JavaScript, arrays can be declared using square brackets `[]`. You can initialize an array with multiple values separated by commas.

```
let fruits = ["Apple", "Banana", "Cherry"];
```

In this example, the `fruits` array contains three elements: `"Apple"`, `"Banana"`, and `"Cherry"`.

Accessing Array Elements:

You can access individual elements of an array by their index. The index of the first element is `0`, the second is `1`, and so on.

```
console.log(fruits[0]);  // Output: Apple
console.log(fruits[1]);  // Output: Banana
console.log(fruits[2]);  // Output: Cherry
```

In this example:

- `fruits[0]` refers to `"Apple"`, which is at index `0`.

Adding Elements:

You can add elements to an array in various ways.

- **Using `push()` to add an element at the end:**

```
fruits.push("Mango");  // Adds "Mango" at the end of the array
console.log(fruits);    // Output: ["Apple", "Banana", "Cherry", "Mango"]
```

- **Using `unshift()` to add an element at the beginning:**

```
fruits.unshift("Orange");  // Adds "Orange" at the start of the array
console.log(fruits);       // Output: ["Orange", "Apple", "Banana", "Cherry",
"Mango"]
```

Loops are often used to iterate through the elements of an array. There are several ways to loop through arrays.

- **Using `for` loop:**

```
for (let i = 0; i < fruits.length; i++) {
  console.log(fruits[i]);   // Output: Apple, Banana, Cherry, Mango
}
```

The `for` loop allows you to iterate through the array using an index variable (`i`). The loop continues until `i` reaches the length of the array.

- **Using `forEach()` method:**

```
fruits.forEach(function(fruit) {
  console.log(fruit);   // Output: Apple, Banana, Cherry, Mango
});
```

The `forEach()` method takes a function as an argument and applies it to each element of the array.

- **Using `map()` method:**

```
fruits.map(function(fruit) {
  console.log(fruit);   // Output: Apple, Banana, Cherry, Mango
});
```

The `map()` method also loops through the array but returns a new array with the results of applying the function to each element.

---

2. Loops in JavaScript

Loops are used to repeat a block of code multiple times. JavaScript provides several types of loops, each with its own use case.

For Loop:

A `for` loop is one of the most common loops. It works by specifying three parts:

1. Initialization (`let i = 0`)
2. Condition (`i < 5`)
3. Increment (`i++`)

```
for (let i = 0; i < 5; i++) {
```

```
  console.log(i);   // Output: 0, 1, 2, 3, 4
}
```

In this example:

- The loop runs 5 times (from 0 to 4).
- Each iteration prints the value of i.

While Loop:

A while loop continues to execute a block of code as long as a specified condition evaluates to true.

```
let i = 0;
while (i < 5) {
  console.log(i);   // Output: 0, 1, 2, 3, 4
  i++;
}
```

The while loop checks the condition (i < 5) before each iteration.

For...of Loop:

The for...of loop is specifically designed for iterating over iterable objects such as arrays, strings, and other collections. It simplifies iteration as it automatically handles the indexing for you.

```
for (let fruit of fruits) {
  console.log(fruit);   // Output: Apple, Banana, Cherry, Mango
}
```

Here, the for...of loop iterates through the fruits array and directly accesses each element (fruit).

---

3. Conditionals in JavaScript

Conditionals are used to perform different actions based on different conditions. JavaScript provides several types of conditional statements for branching logic.

If Statement:

The if statement is used to test a condition. If the condition evaluates to true, the block of code inside the if statement runs.

```
let age = 18;
if (age >= 18) {
```

```
  console.log("Adult");   // Output: Adult
}
```

Here, since `age` is `18`, the condition `age >= 18` evaluates to `true`, and the message `"Adult"` is logged.

Else Statement:

The `else` statement can be used to execute a block of code if the `if` condition evaluates to `false`.

```
let age = 16;
if (age >= 18) {
  console.log("Adult");
} else {
  console.log("Minor");   // Output: Minor
}
```

Since `age` is `16`, which is less than `18`, the `else` block is executed, and `"Minor"` is logged.

Else If Statement:

The `else if` statement allows you to check multiple conditions. If the first condition is `false`, it checks the second condition.

```
let age = 20;
if (age < 18) {
  console.log("Minor");
} else if (age >= 18 && age <= 21) {
  console.log("Young Adult");   // Output: Young Adult
} else {
  console.log("Adult");
}
```

Here, the age `20` satisfies the condition `age >= 18 && age <= 21`, so `"Young Adult"` is logged.

Switch Statement:

The `switch` statement is used to test a variable or expression against multiple cases. It is useful when you have many different conditions to check.

```
let day = 2;
switch (day) {
  case 1:
    console.log("Monday");
    break;
  case 2:
    console.log("Tuesday");   // Output: Tuesday
    break;
```

```
  case 3:
    console.log("Wednesday");
    break;
  default:
    console.log("Invalid Day");
}
```

In this example:

- The value of day is 2, so the second case is matched, and "Tuesday" is printed.
- The break statement is important because it prevents the code from continuing to check other cases.

2. Object-Oriented Programming in JavaScript

Object-Oriented Programming (OOP) is a programming paradigm that organizes code into objects. An object in OOP can contain both **data** (properties) and **functions** (methods) that operate on the data. JavaScript supports OOP and provides several ways to create and manage objects. This approach makes it easier to manage complex systems, allows for reusability, and enhances the maintainability of code.

Let's break down the core concepts of OOP in JavaScript.

1. Creating Objects in JavaScript

In JavaScript, objects can be created using different methods, including **object literals**, **constructor functions**, and **ES6 classes**.

Object Literals:

An object literal is a simple way to define an object. Objects are made up of **key-value pairs**, where each key (or property) maps to a value (which can be a primitive value, array, another object, or function).

Example of creating an object using object literal syntax:

```
let person = {
  name: "John",
  age: 30,
  greet: function() {
    console.log("Hello, " + this.name);
  }
};

person.greet();  // Output: Hello, John
```

In this example:

- name and age are **properties** of the person object.
- greet is a **method** of the object, which uses the this keyword to refer to the current object (person).

---

2. Constructor Functions:

A **constructor function** is a function that is used to create instances of objects that share the same structure. Constructor functions use the this keyword to refer to the new object being created.

Example:

```
function Person(name, age) {
  this.name = name;
  this.age = age;
  this.greet = function() {
    console.log("Hello, " + this.name);
  };
}

let person1 = new Person("Alice", 25);
let person2 = new Person("Bob", 28);

person1.greet();   // Output: Hello, Alice
person2.greet();   // Output: Hello, Bob
```

In this example:

- Person is a constructor function that creates objects with name, age, and a greet method.
- The new keyword is used to create instances of the Person object (person1 and person2).
- The greet method is specific to each object and uses the name property of that object.

---

3. ES6 Classes:

With **ES6 (ECMAScript 2015)**, JavaScript introduced the class syntax to provide a more structured way to define objects and their methods. The class syntax is a more concise and cleaner way to create constructor functions and define methods.

Example:

```
class Person {
  constructor(name, age) {
    this.name = name;
```

```
    this.age = age;
  }

  greet() {
    console.log("Hello, " + this.name);
  }
}

let person1 = new Person("Charlie", 22);
person1.greet();  // Output: Hello, Charlie
```

In this example:

- The `Person` class is defined with a constructor that initializes `name` and `age`.
- The `greet` method is defined inside the class and can be used by instances of `Person`.
- `new Person("Charlie", 22)` creates an instance of the `Person` class with specific values for `name` and `age`.

4. Inheritance in OOP:

JavaScript supports **inheritance**, allowing one class to inherit properties and methods from another class. The `extends` keyword is used to create a subclass, and the `super()` function is used to call the parent class constructor.

Example of Inheritance:
```
class Employee extends Person {
  constructor(name, age, jobTitle) {
    super(name, age);  // Calls the constructor of the Person class
    this.jobTitle = jobTitle;
  }

  work() {
    console.log(this.name + " is working as a " + this.jobTitle);
  }
}

let emp = new Employee("Dave", 35, "Software Developer");
emp.work();  // Output: Dave is working as a Software Developer
```

In this example:

- `Employee` is a subclass of `Person`. It **extends** the `Person` class, meaning it inherits all properties and methods from `Person`.
- The `super()` function is used to call the constructor of the parent (`Person`) class to initialize inherited properties (`name`, `age`).
- The `Employee` class adds a new property (`jobTitle`) and a new method (`work()`).
- The `emp` object is an instance of `Employee`, and it can access both `greet()` (inherited from `Person`) and `work()` (defined in `Employee`).

5. Key Concepts in Object-Oriented Programming (OOP):

- **Encapsulation:** This refers to bundling the data (properties) and methods (functions) that operate on the data into a single unit, or object. JavaScript objects provide encapsulation.
- **Abstraction:** Abstraction refers to hiding the complex implementation details and exposing only the necessary parts of an object. For example, users of an object may interact with its methods without needing to know the internal workings.
- **Polymorphism:** Polymorphism allows objects to take on multiple forms. For instance, a method defined in a parent class can be overridden by a child class, providing a different implementation of that method.
- **Inheritance:** As shown earlier, inheritance allows a class to inherit properties and methods from another class, promoting code reusability.

6. Real-world Example of Object-Oriented Programming:

Let's consider a more real-world example where we define a **Vehicle** class and then create specific vehicle types, such as **Car** and **Motorcycle**.

Example:
```
class Vehicle {
  constructor(make, model) {
    this.make = make;
    this.model = model;
  }

  displayInfo() {
    console.log(`Vehicle Info: ${this.make} ${this.model}`);
  }
}

class Car extends Vehicle {
  constructor(make, model, numDoors) {
    super(make, model);  // Calls the constructor of Vehicle class
    this.numDoors = numDoors;
  }

  displayInfo() {
    console.log(`Car Info: ${this.make} ${this.model}, Doors:
${this.numDoors}`);
  }
}

class Motorcycle extends Vehicle {
  constructor(make, model, type) {
    super(make, model);  // Calls the constructor of Vehicle class
    this.type = type;
  }
```

```
  displayInfo() {
    console.log(`Motorcycle Info: ${this.make} ${this.model}, Type:
${this.type}`);
  }
}

let car = new Car("Toyota", "Camry", 4);
let motorcycle = new Motorcycle("Harley Davidson", "Sportster", "Cruiser");

car.displayInfo();  // Output: Car Info: Toyota Camry, Doors: 4
motorcycle.displayInfo();  // Output: Motorcycle Info: Harley Davidson
Sportster, Type: Cruiser
```

In this example:

- The `Vehicle` class is the base class with common properties (`make`, `model`) and a method (`displayInfo`).
- `Car` and `Motorcycle` are subclasses that extend `Vehicle`. They have their own additional properties (`numDoors`, `type`) and override the `displayInfo()` method to provide specific information for each type of vehicle.

---

3. Error Handling with Try-Catch

Error handling is a critical part of writing robust and reliable JavaScript code. When errors occur in your program, you can use the **try-catch** block to catch and handle them appropriately instead of allowing the program to crash. In addition, JavaScript provides mechanisms for **finally** and **throwing** errors to give you more control over error management.

1. The Try-Catch Block

The **try** block is used to wrap the code that might throw an error. If an error occurs, the control is passed to the **catch** block, where you can handle the error gracefully.

Here's the basic syntax:

```
try {
  // Code that might cause an error
  let result = riskyOperation();
} catch (error) {
  // This block runs if an error occurs
  console.log("An error occurred: " + error.message);
}
```

In this example:

- The `riskyOperation()` function is assumed to be a function that may throw an error.

- If an error occurs within the `try` block, the `catch` block is executed, and the error message is logged to the console.
- The `error` object passed to the `catch` block contains information about the error, such as the error message and stack trace.

Example of Try-Catch:
```
try {
  let result = 10 / 0; // This will not throw an error, but we can simulate
an error condition
} catch (error) {
  console.log("Caught an error: " + error.message); // No error will be
thrown in this case
}
```

Output:

```
Caught an error: Infinity
```

In this example, no actual error occurs because division by zero in JavaScript results in `Infinity`. However, if there was a real error, the `catch` block would handle it.

---

2. The Finally Block

The **finally** block is optional and is always executed, whether or not an error occurred in the `try` block. It is typically used for cleanup operations, such as closing database connections or releasing resources.

Here's the syntax:

```
try {
  let result = riskyOperation();
} catch (error) {
  console.log("Error: " + error.message);
} finally {
  console.log("This runs regardless of an error.");
}
```

In this example:

- The `finally` block executes after the `try` and `catch` blocks, regardless of whether an error was thrown or not.
- It can be useful for code that needs to run after an attempt to execute something, like closing files or cleaning up memory.

Example with Finally:
```
try {
  let result = riskyOperation();
  console.log("Operation was successful.");
```

```
} catch (error) {
  console.log("Caught an error: " + error.message);
} finally {
  console.log("This always runs after the try-catch.");
}
```

Output (if `riskyOperation` succeeds):

```
Operation was successful.
This always runs after the try-catch.
```

Output (if an error occurs in `riskyOperation`):

```
Caught an error: Some error message
This always runs after the try-catch.
```

Even if an error occurs in the `try` block, the `finally` block will always run.

---

3. Throwing Errors with `throw`

In JavaScript, you can **throw** your own errors using the `throw` statement. This is useful when you want to enforce specific conditions in your code and raise custom errors.

Here's an example of how you can throw your own error:

```
function checkAge(age) {
  if (age < 18) {
    throw new Error("You must be at least 18 years old.");
  }
}

try {
  checkAge(15); // This will throw an error
} catch (error) {
  console.log(error.message);  // Output: You must be at least 18 years old.
}
```

In this example:

- The `checkAge()` function checks if the age provided is less than 18.
- If the age is less than 18, an `Error` object is thrown with the message `"You must be at least 18 years old."`
- The `catch` block catches this custom error, and the error message is logged.

Custom Errors:

You can also create more specific error types by using the `Error` constructor or extending the `Error` class to create custom error types.

Example of custom error:

```
class AgeError extends Error {
  constructor(message) {
    super(message);
    this.name = "AgeError"; // Setting the error name
  }
}

function checkAge(age) {
  if (age < 18) {
    throw new AgeError("Age must be 18 or older");
  }
}

try {
  checkAge(15); // This will throw an AgeError
} catch (error) {
  console.log(`${error.name}: ${error.message}`);   // Output: AgeError: Age
must be 18 or older
}
```

In this example:

- We define a custom error class `AgeError` that extends the built-in `Error` class.
- When the age is less than 18, the `AgeError` is thrown, and the catch block logs the error's name and message.

---

4. Best Practices for Error Handling

1. **Be Specific with Error Messages:** When throwing errors, provide meaningful error messages that explain what went wrong and, if possible, how to fix it.
2. **Use Finally for Cleanup:** Always use the `finally` block for cleanup tasks, such as closing resources or resetting states, regardless of whether an error occurred.
3. **Avoid Catching Unnecessary Errors:** Don't catch errors unless you plan to handle them. Catching all errors without acting on them can hide bugs and make debugging difficult.
4. **Log Errors for Debugging:** When an error occurs, logging it with detailed information (including stack trace) helps developers debug and understand what went wrong.
5. **Throw Specific Errors:** Instead of throwing generic errors, use or create specific error types that help identify different kinds of issues (e.g., `ValidationError`, `NetworkError`, `DatabaseError`).

4. Using JavaScript Libraries (e.g., jQuery) for Enhanced Functionality

JavaScript libraries, such as **jQuery**, are pre-written code that can help simplify and accelerate the development process. They abstract away common JavaScript operations and provide simple, easy-to-use functions for performing complex tasks. By leveraging such libraries, developers can focus more on application logic rather than reinventing the wheel for common tasks.

What is jQuery?

jQuery is a fast, lightweight, and feature-rich JavaScript library. It was created to simplify the process of working with HTML documents, handling events, performing animations, and making asynchronous requests with AJAX. It works across all browsers and has been one of the most popular JavaScript libraries for many years.

Features of jQuery:

1. **DOM Manipulation:** jQuery makes it easy to select and modify elements in the DOM (Document Object Model).
2. **Event Handling:** Simplifies binding and handling of user events like clicks, mouse movements, and keyboard input.
3. **Animations and Effects:** Provides built-in functions for animating page elements (e.g., hiding/showing elements, fading).
4. **AJAX Support:** Simplifies making asynchronous requests to a server to fetch data without reloading the page.
5. **Cross-Browser Compatibility:** jQuery handles many of the quirks between different browsers and ensures that the same code works across all of them.

---

1. Including jQuery

Before using jQuery, you must include it in your project. You can either download and host the jQuery file locally or link to a Content Delivery Network (CDN) version. Here's how you include jQuery via a CDN:

```
<script src="https://code.jquery.com/jquery-3.6.0.min.js"></script>
```

You can place this `<script>` tag in the `<head>` or just before the closing `</body>` tag in your HTML document. The CDN approach is often preferred because it is fast and ensures that the browser may already have a cached version of jQuery if other websites are using the same CDN.

---

2. DOM Manipulation with jQuery

jQuery simplifies the process of accessing and manipulating elements on your web page. For instance, you can easily select elements by their ID, class, or other attributes, and then perform various actions on them.

Common DOM Manipulation Operations with jQuery:

- **Selecting Elements:** To select elements, use the $ function, followed by a selector (similar to CSS selectors).

```
// Select an element by ID
$('#myElement')  // Selects the element with id="myElement"

// Select elements by class
$('.myClass')    // Selects all elements with class="myClass"

// Select all elements of a certain tag
$('div')         // Selects all <div> elements on the page
```

- **Modifying Content:** jQuery provides simple methods for changing the content of selected elements.

```
// Change the text content of an element with id="myElement"
$('#myElement').text('New Text');

// Change the HTML content of an element
$('#myElement').html('<p>New HTML Content</p>');
```

- **CSS Manipulation:** You can easily change the CSS properties of elements.

```
// Change the background color of an element
$('#myElement').css('background-color', 'blue');
```

- **Hiding/Showing Elements:** jQuery has built-in methods to hide or show elements smoothly.

```
// Hide an element
$('#myElement').hide();

// Show an element
$('#myElement').show();

// Toggle visibility of an element
$('#myElement').toggle();
```

Example: DOM Manipulation with jQuery

```
<button id="myButton">Click Me</button>
<div id="message">Hello, World!</div>

<script>
  // Change the message text when the button is clicked
```

```
$('#myButton').click(function() {
  $('#message').text('You clicked the button!');
});
</script>
```

In this example, when the button with ID `myButton` is clicked, the text content of the `#message` div is changed.

---

3. Event Handling with jQuery

One of the most powerful features of jQuery is its simple and consistent event handling mechanism. It allows developers to bind event handlers (like click, hover, or keypress) to DOM elements.

Common jQuery Event Handlers:

- **Click Event:**

```
$('#myButton').click(function() {
  alert('Button clicked!');
});
```

- **Mouseover Event:**

```
$('#myElement').mouseover(function() {
  $(this).css('color', 'red');  // Change text color to red when mouse hovers over the element
});
```

- **Keydown Event:**

```
$(document).keydown(function(event) {
  console.log('Key pressed: ' + event.key);  // Logs the key pressed
});
```

- **Submit Event:**

```
$('#myForm').submit(function(event) {
  event.preventDefault();  // Prevents form from submitting
  alert('Form submitted!');
});
```

Example: Event Handling with jQuery
```
<button id="alertButton">Click me</button>

<script>
  // Show an alert when the button is clicked
```

```
$('#alertButton').click(function() {
  alert('You clicked the button!');
});
</script>
```

In this example, clicking the `#alertButton` will trigger the alert popup.

4. AJAX Requests with jQuery

AJAX (Asynchronous JavaScript and XML) allows you to send and receive data from a server asynchronously (i.e., without refreshing the entire page). jQuery simplifies AJAX requests with methods like `$.ajax()`, `$.get()`, and `$.post()`.

Example of an AJAX Request with jQuery:
```
$.ajax({
  url: 'https://api.example.com/data',   // API endpoint to fetch data from
  method: 'GET',                          // HTTP method
  success: function(response) {           // Handle successful response
    console.log(response);                // Output data to the console
  },
  error: function() {                     // Handle any errors
    console.log('Error occurred');
  }
});
```

- The `url` specifies the API endpoint or server resource.
- The `method` specifies the type of request (e.g., GET, POST).
- The `success` function is executed if the request is successful, and the `response` parameter contains the server's response.
- The `error` function is executed if there is an error in the request.

Simplified AJAX with jQuery:
```
$.get('https://api.example.com/data', function(data) {
  console.log(data);   // Process the data received from the server
});
```

This code sends a GET request and logs the response when the data is received.

5. Advantages of Using jQuery

- **Cross-Browser Compatibility:** jQuery handles the inconsistencies between different browsers (e.g., Internet Explorer, Chrome, Firefox, etc.), ensuring your code works seamlessly across all platforms.
- **Concise and Readable Syntax:** jQuery syntax is cleaner and more concise, making it easier to write and maintain code.

- **Rich Set of Built-In Features:** jQuery includes a wide range of built-in methods for DOM manipulation, event handling, animations, and AJAX.
- **Improves Development Speed:** By abstracting away common tasks, jQuery helps developers implement functionality faster and more efficiently.

5. Debugging and Troubleshooting JavaScript Code

Debugging is an essential aspect of programming that involves identifying and fixing issues in the code to ensure it functions correctly. In JavaScript, there are various techniques and tools available to help developers troubleshoot their code. Below, we explore some of the most effective debugging strategies and tools that can help you resolve errors and enhance the quality of your JavaScript code.

1. Using `console.log()` for Debugging

The simplest and most commonly used method for debugging JavaScript is using `console.log()`. This allows you to log variables, objects, or messages to the console so you can track the flow of your code and the values of different expressions during execution.

How to Use `console.log()`
```
let x = 10;
console.log(x);   // Output: 10
```

You can use `console.log()` to output:

- Variables
- Expressions
- Objects (e.g., arrays, functions, or complex objects)
- The flow of the code

Example of Debugging with `console.log()`
```
function add(a, b) {
    console.log("a:", a); // Debugging variable a
    console.log("b:", b); // Debugging variable b
    return a + b;
}

let result = add(5, 3);
console.log("Result:", result); // Output the result
```

This will print the values of `a`, `b`, and `result` at different points in the execution, helping you verify that the function is working as expected.

2. Using Browser's Developer Tools

Modern browsers like Chrome, Firefox, and Edge come with built-in developer tools that make debugging JavaScript much easier. These tools allow you to inspect the DOM, network requests, and JavaScript execution in real-time.

How to Access Developer Tools

- **Chrome/Edge/Firefox:** Press `F12` or `Ctrl + Shift + I` (Windows) / `Cmd + Option + I` (Mac) to open the developer tools.
- **Safari:** Enable the Developer menu in Safari preferences, then press `Cmd + Option + I`.

Key Features in Developer Tools for Debugging

- **Console Tab:** The Console tab allows you to view all `console.log()` outputs, warnings, and errors generated by your JavaScript code. You can also execute JavaScript directly in the console for quick testing.
- **Sources Tab:** In the Sources tab, you can inspect the JavaScript files used on your webpage. Here, you can set breakpoints to pause code execution and step through your code line by line.
  - **Breakpoints:** A breakpoint allows you to pause the execution of your code at a specific line. You can inspect the state of variables, the call stack, and the flow of execution. Breakpoints are essential for identifying exactly where and why a particular issue occurs.
  - **Step-through Debugging:** After hitting a breakpoint, you can step through the code line by line to observe how data changes or how logic flows.

---

3. Breakpoints and Step-through Debugging

Breakpoints and step-through debugging are some of the most powerful techniques available in modern browser developer tools.

How to Set a Breakpoint

1. Open the **Sources** tab in the browser's Developer Tools.
2. Find the file that contains the code you want to debug.
3. Click on the line number where you want to set the breakpoint (the line turns blue, indicating a breakpoint is set).
4. Reload the page or trigger the code execution, and the browser will pause at the breakpoint.

Stepping Through Code

Once the code execution is paused at a breakpoint, you can:

- **Step Over**: Move to the next line of code in the same function.

- **Step Into**: Go into the function called on the current line to see how it works.
- **Step Out**: Exit the current function and go back to the calling function.
- **Resume**: Continue execution until the next breakpoint is encountered.

This allows you to examine how the program executes and how the values of variables change as the code runs.

---

4. Error Stack Traces

When an error occurs in JavaScript, the browser usually logs a **stack trace** to the console. The stack trace provides important information about where the error occurred and the sequence of function calls leading up to it.

Understanding a Stack Trace

A stack trace typically includes:

- The function name(s) where the error occurred.
- The file name(s) and line number(s) where the error occurred.
- The order of function calls that led to the error.

Example of Stack Trace
```
function calculate(x, y) {
    return x / y;
}

function processData() {
    let result = calculate(10, 0); // Division by zero
}

processData();
```

In the example above, calling `processData()` will cause an error (division by zero). The console will show an error like this:

```
Uncaught Error: Division by zero
    at calculate (script.js:2)
    at processData (script.js:6)
    at script.js:9
```

The stack trace shows:

- The error occurred in the `calculate` function at line 2.
- The `processData` function called `calculate` at line 6.
- The error was triggered in the script at line 9.

By examining the stack trace, you can identify exactly where the issue occurred and which function was involved.

5. Using `try-catch` for Error Handling

The `try-catch` block in JavaScript allows you to handle errors gracefully and prevent them from crashing your entire application. You can wrap potentially problematic code inside a `try` block, and if an error occurs, it will be caught by the `catch` block, allowing you to handle it.

Basic `try-catch` Syntax
```
try {
    let result = riskyFunction();
} catch (error) {
    console.log("Error: " + error.message);   // Log the error message
} finally {
    console.log("This will always run");
}
```

- The `try` block contains code that may throw an error.
- The `catch` block handles the error if one occurs.
- The `finally` block runs after the `try` and `catch` blocks, regardless of whether an error occurred or not. This is useful for cleanup tasks like closing file streams or releasing resources.

Example: Using `try-catch`
```
function checkAge(age) {
    if (age < 18) {
        throw new Error("You must be at least 18 years old.");
    } else {
        console.log("Age is valid.");
    }
}

try {
    checkAge(16);   // This will throw an error
} catch (error) {
    console.log(error.message);   // Output: You must be at least 18 years old.
}
```

In this example, the `checkAge` function throws an error if the age is less than 18. The `try-catch` block catches that error and logs the error message instead of crashing the application.

6. Common Debugging Techniques

- **Isolate the Problem**: If your code isn't working as expected, try isolating the problem by commenting out sections of the code or using `console.log()` to check intermediate values. This will help you focus on the section that's causing the issue.
- **Check for Syntax Errors**: JavaScript is very particular about syntax. Even a small mistake like missing a semicolon, bracket, or quotation mark can cause an error. Browsers often provide clear error messages pointing to the specific line with the issue.
- **Revisit Logic**: Sometimes, the issue is not with the code structure but with the logic. Take a step back, review your logic, and verify that it behaves as expected.
- **Use Debugging Tools**: Use the browser's built-in debugger or a third-party tool like **Visual Studio Code**'s integrated debugger to set breakpoints, inspect variables, and step through your code in real-time.

These topics cover the fundamental concepts of JavaScript development, from basic operations with arrays and loops to advanced techniques like object-oriented programming and debugging. Understanding these concepts will help you become proficient in writing efficient, maintainable, and error-free JavaScript code.

Practical Questions & Answers

Arrays, Loops, and Conditionals

1. **Q: How do you create an array of numbers from 1 to 5 in JavaScript?**
   - **A:**

     ```
     let numbers = [1, 2, 3, 4, 5];
     ```

2. **Q: How do you access the first element of an array in JavaScript?**
   - **A:**

     ```
     let arr = [10, 20, 30];
     console.log(arr[0]);  // Output: 10
     ```

3. **Q: How can you loop through an array using a `for` loop?**
   - **A:**

     ```
     let fruits = ["Apple", "Banana", "Cherry"];
     for (let i = 0; i < fruits.length; i++) {
         console.log(fruits[i]);
     }
     ```

4. **Q: What is the purpose of the `continue` statement in a loop?**
   - **A:** The `continue` statement skips the current iteration and proceeds to the next iteration of the loop. For example:

```
for (let i = 0; i < 5; i++) {
    if (i === 3) continue;  // Skip when i is 3
    console.log(i);  // Output: 0, 1, 2, 4
}
```

5. **Q: How do you check if an element is present in an array using `includes()`?**
   - **A:**

   ```
   let arr = [10, 20, 30];
   console.log(arr.includes(20));  // Output: true
   ```

6. **Q: How can you loop through an array using `forEach()`?**
   - **A:**

   ```
   let colors = ["Red", "Green", "Blue"];
   colors.forEach(function(color) {
       console.log(color);
   });
   ```

7. **Q: How can you implement a conditional statement to check if a number is even or odd?**
   - **A:**

   ```
   let number = 4;
   if (number % 2 === 0) {
       console.log("Even");
   } else {
       console.log("Odd");
   }
   ```

8. **Q: Write a `switch` statement to display the day of the week based on a number.**
   - **A:**

   ```
   let day = 2;
   switch (day) {
       case 1:
           console.log("Monday");
           break;
       case 2:
           console.log("Tuesday");
           break;
       default:
           console.log("Invalid day");
   }
   ```

9. **Q: How do you use a `while` loop to print numbers from 1 to 5?**
   - **A:**

   ```
   let i = 1;
   while (i <= 5) {
       console.log(i);
       i++;
   ```

```
}
```

10. **Q: How would you find the index of an element in an array?**
    o **A:**

    ```
    let arr = ["a", "b", "c"];
    console.log(arr.indexOf("b"));   // Output: 1
    ```

Object-Oriented Programming in JavaScript

11. **Q: How do you create an object in JavaScript with properties `name` and `age`?**
    o **A:**

    ```
    let person = {
        name: "John",
        age: 30
    };
    ```

12. **Q: How do you define a method in an object to greet someone?**
    o **A:**

    ```
    let person = {
        name: "John",
        greet: function() {
            console.log("Hello, " + this.name);
        }
    };
    person.greet();   // Output: Hello, John
    ```

13. **Q: How do you create a constructor function to make multiple instances of an object?**
    o **A:**

    ```
    function Person(name, age) {
        this.name = name;
        this.age = age;
    }
    let person1 = new Person("Alice", 25);
    let person2 = new Person("Bob", 30);
    console.log(person1.name);   // Output: Alice
    ```

14. **Q: How do you create a subclass in JavaScript using `class` and `extends`?**
    o **A:**

    ```
    class Animal {
        constructor(name) {
            this.name = name;
        }
        speak() {
            console.log(this.name + " makes a sound.");
        }
    ```

```
    }

class Dog extends Animal {
    speak() {
        console.log(this.name + " barks.");
    }
}

let dog = new Dog("Buddy");
dog.speak();   // Output: Buddy barks.
```

15. **Q: How do you use `super()` in a subclass constructor?**
   o **A:**

```
class Animal {
    constructor(name) {
        this.name = name;
    }
}

class Dog extends Animal {
    constructor(name, breed) {
        super(name);   // Call parent constructor
        this.breed = breed;
    }
}

let dog = new Dog("Buddy", "Golden Retriever");
console.log(dog.name);   // Output: Buddy
console.log(dog.breed);   // Output: Golden Retriever
```

Error Handling with Try-Catch

16. **Q: How do you handle an error in JavaScript using `try-catch`?**
   o **A:**

```
try {
    let result = riskyFunction();
} catch (error) {
    console.log("Error occurred: " + error.message);
}
```

17. **Q: How can you manually throw an error in JavaScript?**
   o **A:**

```
function checkAge(age) {
    if (age < 18) {
        throw new Error("You must be at least 18 years old.");
    }
}

try {
    checkAge(16);
```

```
} catch (error) {
    console.log(error.message);   // Output: You must be at least
18 years old.
}
```

18. **Q: What is the purpose of the `finally` block in `try-catch`?**
    - ○ **A:** The `finally` block is used to execute code that needs to run regardless of whether an error occurred or not.

    ```
    try {
        let result = riskyFunction();
    } catch (error) {
        console.log("Error: " + error.message);
    } finally {
        console.log("This runs no matter what.");
    }
    ```

Using JavaScript Libraries (e.g., jQuery) for Enhanced Functionality

19. **Q: How do you include jQuery in your HTML file?**
    - ○ **A:**

    ```
    <script src="https://code.jquery.com/jquery-
    3.6.0.min.js"></script>
    ```

20. **Q: How do you use jQuery to hide an element when a button is clicked?**
    - ○ **A:**

    ```
    <button id="myButton">Hide</button>
    <div id="myDiv">This is a div.</div>

    <script>
        $('#myButton').click(function() {
            $('#myDiv').hide();
        });
    </script>
    ```

Bonus Practical Question on Debugging

21. **Q: How do you use `console.log()` to debug a function that is not returning the expected value?**
    - ○ **A:**

    ```
    function add(a, b) {
        console.log("a:", a);   // Debugging a
        console.log("b:", b);   // Debugging b
        return a + b;
    }

    let result = add(5, 3);   // Check the logs for debugging
    ```

```
console.log(result);   // Output: 8
```

30 multiple-choice questions (MCQs)

Arrays, Loops, and Conditionals

1. **Which of the following is the correct way to declare an array in JavaScript?**
    - A) `let fruits = {apple, banana, cherry}`
    - B) `let fruits = ["apple", "banana", "cherry"]`
    - C) `let fruits = ("apple", "banana", "cherry")`
    - D) `let fruits = {1: "apple", 2: "banana", 3: "cherry"}`

    Answer: B) `let fruits = ["apple", "banana", "cherry"]`

2. **How do you access the third element of an array `let arr = [10, 20, 30, 40];`?**
    - A) `arr[3]`
    - B) `arr[2]`
    - C) `arr[1]`
    - D) `arr(3)`

    Answer: B) `arr[2]`

3. **Which of the following methods will add an item to the end of an array?**
    - A) `array.unshift()`
    - B) `array.push()`
    - C) `array.pop()`
    - D) `array.shift()`

    Answer: B) `array.push()`

4. **What is the output of the following code?** `let nums = [1, 2, 3];` `console.log(nums.length);`
    - A) 2
    - B) 3
    - C) 1
    - D) `undefined`

    Answer: B) 3

5. **How do you create a loop that will print numbers 1 through 5?**
    - A)

      ```
      for (let i = 1; i < 6; i++) { console.log(i); }
      ```

    - B)

      ```
      for (let i = 0; i <= 5; i++) { console.log(i); }
      ```

    - C)

      ```
      while (i < 5) { console.log(i); i++; }
      ```

○ D) All of the above
Answer: D) All of the above

6. **Which loop is best for iterating over an array of elements?**
   ○ A) `for`
   ○ B) `while`
   ○ C) `forEach`
   ○ D) `do...while`
   Answer: C) `forEach`

7. **What will be the output of the following code?** `let num = 10; if (num > 5) {`
   `console.log("Yes"); } else { console.log("No"); }`
   ○ A) `No`
   ○ B) `Yes`
   ○ C) `undefined`
   ○ D) `error`
   Answer: B) `Yes`

8. **Which of the following is the correct way to write a `switch` statement for a variable `day` with 3 possible values: 1, 2, 3?**
   ○ A)

   ```
   switch (day) {
       case 1:
           console.log("Monday");
           break;
       case 2:
           console.log("Tuesday");
           break;
       case 3:
           console.log("Wednesday");
           break;
       default:
           console.log("Invalid day");
   }
   ```

   ○ B)

   ```
   switch (day) {
       case "Monday":
           console.log(1);
           break;
   }
   ```

   ○ C) `if` statements with `else if`
   ○ D) Both A and C
   Answer: A) Correct `switch` syntax

Object-Oriented Programming in JavaScript

9. **How do you create a class in JavaScript?**

o A)

```
class Car {
    constructor(make, model) {
        this.make = make;
        this.model = model;
    }
}
```

o B)

```
function Car(make, model) {
    this.make = make;
    this.model = model;
}
```

o C)

```
var Car = { make: 'Toyota', model: 'Camry' };
```

o D) All of the above
Answer: A) Correct class syntax

10. **What does the `this` keyword refer to inside a method in a class?**
    o A) The function in which `this` is defined
    o B) The object that the method belongs to
    o C) The parent class
    o D) The global object
    Answer: B) The object that the method belongs to

11. **What is inheritance in JavaScript?**
    o A) A feature that allows an object to inherit properties and methods from another object
    o B) A function that modifies an object's properties
    o C) The process of changing an object's constructor
    o D) A method to make a property public or private
    Answer: A) A feature that allows an object to inherit properties and methods from another object

12. **How do you use inheritance in JavaScript?**
    o A)

```
class Car extends Vehicle { ... }
```

o B)

```
class Car = new Vehicle();
```

o C)

```
Car.prototype = Object.create(Vehicle);
```

- o D) None of the above

  Answer: A) `extends` keyword for inheritance

13. **What is the purpose of the `constructor` method in JavaScript classes?**
    - o A) To create a new object
    - o B) To initialize the properties of an object
    - o C) To call parent class methods
    - o D) To perform error handling

    Answer: B) To initialize the properties of an object

14. **How would you create an object from a class in JavaScript?**
    - o A) `let obj = new ClassName();`
    - o B) `let obj = ClassName.create();`
    - o C) `let obj = createClass();`
    - o D) `let obj = new ClassName {}`

    Answer: A) `let obj = new ClassName();`

Error Handling with Try-Catch

15. **What does the `try` block in JavaScript do?**
    - o A) It specifies the code to be executed when an error occurs.
    - o B) It allows you to define code that is protected from errors.
    - o C) It is used to create a custom error.
    - o D) It executes code regardless of errors.

    Answer: B) It allows you to define code that is protected from errors.

16. **What happens if an error occurs inside a `try` block and there is no `catch` block?**
    - o A) The program crashes
    - o B) The error is ignored
    - o C) A default error message is displayed
    - o D) The program stops executing

    Answer: A) The program crashes

17. **What is the purpose of the `finally` block in error handling?**
    - o A) It ensures that the code inside it is always executed, whether there is an error or not.
    - o B) It allows you to rethrow an error after catching it.
    - o C) It handles runtime errors.
    - o D) It prints error messages to the console.

    Answer: A) It ensures that the code inside it is always executed, whether there is an error or not.

18. **How can you throw a custom error in JavaScript?**
    - o A)

      ```
      throw new Error("Something went wrong!");
      ```

    - o B)

      ```
      throw "Error message";
      ```

- C)

  ```
  customError("Error");
  ```

- D) Both A and B
  Answer: D) Both A and B

Using JavaScript Libraries (e.g., jQuery) for Enhanced Functionality

19. **How do you include jQuery in your HTML file?**
    - A) `<script src="jquery.js"></script>`
    - B) `<script src="https://code.jquery.com/jquery-3.6.0.min.js"></script>`
    - C) `<script>import jQuery from 'jquery'</script>`
    - D) All of the above
      Answer: B) `<script src="https://code.jquery.com/jquery-3.6.0.min.js"></script>`

20. **How do you select an element with the ID `myDiv` using jQuery?**
    - A) `$("#myDiv")`
    - B) `document.querySelector("#myDiv")`
    - C) `getElementById("myDiv")`
    - D) Both A and B
      Answer: A) `$("#myDiv")`

21. **How do you hide an element using jQuery?**
    - A) `$("#myElement").hide();`
    - B) `$("#myElement").display = "none";`
    - C) `$("#myElement").visibility = "hidden";`
    - D) `$("#myElement").remove();`
      Answer: A) `$("#myElement").hide();`

22. **How do you make an AJAX request with jQuery?**
    - A)

      ```
      $.ajax({
          url: 'https://api.example.com/data',
          method: 'GET',
          success: function(response) { console.log(response); },
          error: function() { console.log("Error!"); }
      });
      ```

    - B)

      ```
      $.request({
          url: 'https://api.example.com/data'
      });
      ```

    - C)

```
jQuery.get('https://api.example.com/data', function(response) {
console.log(response); });
```

- o D) Both A and C
  Answer: D) Both A and C

Debugging and Troubleshooting JavaScript Code

23. **What is the purpose of `console.log()` in JavaScript?**
    - o A) To log errors to the console
    - o B) To display values in the console for debugging
    - o C) To stop the script from running
    - o D) To trigger an exception

    Answer: B) To display values in the console for debugging

24. **Which of the following is used to open the Developer Tools in most browsers?**
    - o A) `Ctrl + P`
    - o B) `F12` or `Ctrl + Shift + I`
    - o C) `Ctrl + Alt + D`
    - o D) `Shift + F5`

    Answer: B) `F12` or `Ctrl + Shift + I`

25. **How do you set a breakpoint in the browser's Developer Tools?**
    - o A) Right-click on the code and select "Set Breakpoint"
    - o B) Click on the "Sources" tab and click on the line number
    - o C) Press `Ctrl + B`
    - o D) Both A and B

    Answer: B) Click on the "Sources" tab and click on the line number

26. **Which statement is true about the `debugger` keyword?**
    - o A) It forces the browser to open the Developer Tools.
    - o B) It causes the script to stop execution and enter debugging mode.
    - o C) It throws an error.
    - o D) It automatically fixes bugs.

    Answer: B) It causes the script to stop execution and enter debugging mode.

27. **What is a stack trace in JavaScript?**
    - o A) A list of all variables in memory
    - o B) A detailed error report showing the path of execution
    - o C) The number of lines in the JavaScript file
    - o D) The number of errors in the program

    Answer: B) A detailed error report showing the path of execution

28. **What should you do if you encounter a `null` value in your JavaScript code?**
    - o A) Continue coding, JavaScript will handle it.
    - o B) Check if the variable was properly initialized before use.
    - o C) Delete the variable.
    - o D) Throw an error explicitly.

    Answer: B) Check if the variable was properly initialized before use.

29. **Which tool is best for inspecting live DOM elements while debugging?**
    - ○ A) Node.js
    - ○ B) Browser Developer Tools (Elements Tab)
    - ○ C) Visual Studio Code
    - ○ D) Webpack

      Answer: B) Browser Developer Tools (Elements Tab)

30. **What will the following code do:** `try { let x = undefinedVar; } catch (e) { console.log(e); }?`
    - ○ A) Logs `undefinedVar`
    - ○ B) Logs an error message with the exception details
    - ○ C) Does nothing
    - ○ D) Throws an uncaught exception

      Answer: B) Logs an error message with the exception details

50 short questions and answers

Arrays, Loops, and Conditionals

1. **Q: How do you declare an array in JavaScript?**
   A: `let arr = [1, 2, 3, 4];`

2. **Q: How can you access the second element of an array `arr = [10, 20, 30]`?**
   A: `arr[1]`

3. **Q: What method adds an element to the end of an array?**
   A: `push()`

4. **Q: How do you iterate through an array using a `for` loop?**
   A:

   ```
   for (let i = 0; i < arr.length; i++) {
       console.log(arr[i]);
   }
   ```

5. **Q: How do you create a `while` loop that prints numbers from 1 to 5?**
   A:

   ```
   let i = 1;
   while (i <= 5) {
       console.log(i);
       i++;
   }
   ```

6. **Q: What is the output of `let num = 4; if (num > 5) { console.log("Greater"); } else { console.log("Smaller"); }?`**
   A: `Smaller`

7. **Q: How do you write a `switch` statement for days of the week?**
   A:

```
switch(day) {
    case 1: console.log("Monday"); break;
    case 2: console.log("Tuesday"); break;
    default: console.log("Invalid day");
}
```

8. **Q: What is the syntax to loop through an array using `forEach()`?**
   A:

```
arr.forEach(item => console.log(item));
```

9. **Q: How do you add an item to the beginning of an array?**
   A: `arr.unshift(item)`
10. **Q: What is the syntax of an `if` statement?**
    A:

```
if (condition) {
    // code to execute
}
```

Object-Oriented Programming in JavaScript

11. **Q: How do you create an object in JavaScript?**
    A:

```
let person = { name: "John", age: 30 };
```

12. **Q: What keyword is used to create an instance of a class in JavaScript?**
    A: `new`
13. **Q: How do you define a constructor method in a class?**
    A:

```
class Person {
    constructor(name, age) {
        this.name = name;
        this.age = age;
    }
}
```

14. **Q: How do you create inheritance in JavaScript classes?**
    A: `class Child extends Parent {}`
15. **Q: What does the `this` keyword refer to in an object method?**
    A: `this` refers to the current object.

16. **Q: How do you define a method inside a class?**
   A:

```
class Person {
    greet() {
        console.log("Hello");
    }
}
```

17. **Q: What is encapsulation in JavaScript OOP?**
   A: Encapsulation is the concept of bundling data (properties) and methods that operate on the data within one unit (class).

18. **Q: How do you call a parent class method in a subclass?**
   A: `super.methodName()`

19. **Q: What is the purpose of the `constructor()` method in a class?**
   A: The constructor method initializes the object's properties when an instance is created.

20. **Q: How do you create a new instance of an object from a class?**
   A: `let obj = new ClassName();`

Error Handling with Try-Catch

21. **Q: What does the `try` block do in error handling?**
   A: It contains code that might throw an error.

22. **Q: What is the role of the `catch` block?**
   A: It handles any errors thrown by the `try` block.

23. **Q: How do you throw a custom error in JavaScript?**
   A: `throw new Error("Custom error message");`

24. **Q: What happens if an error occurs in the `try` block but there is no `catch` block?**
   A: The program will stop executing, and an unhandled error will be thrown.

25. **Q: What is the `finally` block used for?**
   A: The `finally` block is used to execute code regardless of whether an error occurred or not.

26. **Q: What will the following code output: `try { throw "Error"; } catch (e) { console.log(e); }`?**
   A: `Error`

27. **Q: Can you have multiple `catch` blocks in a `try-catch` statement?**
   A: No, JavaScript only allows one `catch` block.

28. **Q: How do you catch a specific error type in a `try-catch` block?**
   A: Use an `if` condition inside the `catch` block to check the error type.

29. **Q: What does `console.error()` do?**
   A: It prints an error message to the console, often with a stack trace.

30. **Q: Can you use `throw` to create a custom exception?**
   A: Yes, `throw` is used to manually generate errors or exceptions.

Using JavaScript Libraries (e.g., jQuery) for Enhanced Functionality

31. **Q: How do you include the jQuery library in your HTML?**
    A: `<script src="https://code.jquery.com/jquery-3.6.0.min.js"></script>`

32. **Q: How do you hide an element with the ID `myDiv` using jQuery?**
    A: `$("#myDiv").hide();`

33. **Q: What does the jQuery method `$('#myElement').text('Hello')` do?**
    A: It sets the text content of the element with ID `myElement` to "Hello".

34. **Q: How do you select all paragraphs on a page using jQuery?**
    A: `$("p")`

35. **Q: How do you make an AJAX GET request using jQuery?**
    A:

```
$.ajax({
    url: 'example.com',
    method: 'GET',
    success: function(data) { console.log(data); }
});
```

36. **Q: How do you add a click event listener to a button with jQuery?**
    A: `$('#myButton').click(function() { alert("Button clicked!"); });`

37. **Q: What is the purpose of `$(document).ready()` in jQuery?**
    A: It ensures the DOM is fully loaded before executing the JavaScript code.

38. **Q: How can you change the CSS of an element using jQuery?**
    A: `$('#element').css('color', 'blue');`

39. **Q: How do you append a new element to a div using jQuery?**
    A: `$('#myDiv').append('<p>New paragraph</p>');`

40. **Q: How can you show a hidden element using jQuery?**
    A: `$('#myElement').show();`

Debugging and Troubleshooting JavaScript Code

41. **Q: What is the simplest way to debug JavaScript code?**
    A: Using `console.log()` to print variable values and check the flow.

42. **Q: How can you open the Developer Tools in most browsers?**
    A: Press `F12` or `Ctrl + Shift + I`.

43. **Q: What does the `debugger` keyword do in JavaScript?**
    A: It pauses the code execution and opens the debugger in the browser.

44. **Q: What does a stack trace provide during debugging?**
    A: It shows the sequence of function calls leading to an error.

45. **Q: How do you step through code in the browser's Developer Tools?**
    A: Set breakpoints and use the step-through options in the Sources tab.

46. **Q: How can you find the source of an error in JavaScript?**
    A: Use the error message and stack trace from the console.

47. **Q: What is the purpose of `console.warn()`?**

A: It prints a warning message to the console, usually indicating potential issues.

48. **Q: What should you do when you encounter a `null` value in your code?**

A: Check if the variable was initialized correctly before using it.

49. **Q: How do you resolve `undefined` errors in JavaScript?**

A: Ensure that variables are declared and initialized before usage.

50. **Q: What is the advantage of using breakpoints in debugging?**

A: They allow you to pause the code at specific points and inspect the state of variables.

CHAPTER 6: BRINGING IT ALL TOGETHER: BUILDING YOUR FIRST WEB PAGE

Building your first web page is an exciting and rewarding process. It involves several steps, from planning your page layout to testing and debugging your code. Let's break down each step to understand how you can create a functional, interactive, and responsive web page.

---

1. Planning Your Web Page Layout

Planning your web page layout is a crucial first step in building a website. It ensures that your website is not only functional but also user-friendly and visually appealing. A well-organized layout provides a smooth navigation experience and encourages users to engage with the content. Below, we'll delve into the key considerations you need to make when planning the layout of your web page.

---

1. Purpose and Content

Before you start designing your web page, it's important to understand the **purpose** of the website. This helps you determine what content should be included and how it should be presented. The type of website you are building will influence the design and layout. Here are a few examples of how different types of websites might approach content:

- **Personal Portfolio**: If you're creating a portfolio website, your content will likely include a bio, a list of projects, and perhaps a contact form. The layout should highlight your work and professional achievements.
- **Blog**: A blog website typically contains posts organized by categories, archives, and tags. The layout should facilitate easy reading, navigation between posts, and easy discovery of related content.
- **Product Page**: A product page might include product details, images, pricing information, and a call-to-action button (like "Buy Now"). The layout must focus on displaying the product in an appealing and easy-to-understand way.

When planning your content:

- **Content Types**: Identify the types of content you need to display, such as text, images, videos, forms, charts, etc.
- **Content Structure**: Think about how to organize the content for easy readability. For example, using headings, paragraphs, and bullet points to break down text-heavy sections.
- **User Goals**: Understand what action you want the user to take on the page. Should they fill out a form, purchase a product, or simply read an article? Your layout should encourage users to take that action.

---

2. Wireframes

Wireframing is the process of creating a visual blueprint of your web page layout. It helps you outline the structure of your page before adding design elements like colors, fonts, and images. A wireframe is usually a low-fidelity representation of your website, focusing on the structure and placement of key elements.

- **Hand-drawn Wireframes**: You can start by sketching out your page layout on paper. This is a fast, low-cost way to explore different layout options and understand how the content will flow.
- **Digital Wireframes**: You can use digital tools like Figma, Sketch, Adobe XD, or even free tools like Balsamiq to create a more refined wireframe. These tools allow for easier edits and collaboration if you're working with a team.

Wireframes typically include:

- **Header**: The top section, which may include the website logo, title, and navigation links.
- **Content Area**: The main part of the page that holds the text, images, or other media.
- **Sidebar**: If used, this is typically a vertical column that may contain additional content or links.
- **Footer**: The section at the bottom of the page that usually contains copyright information, links, or other smaller sections.

Wireframing helps visualize how the page will look once the content is added. It also allows you to easily rearrange sections and make adjustments to the layout before implementing it.

---

3. Layout Components

When planning your web page layout, you'll need to decide on the key **components** that should be included. Each of these components plays a critical role in the structure and flow of your website.

a. Header

The **header** is usually at the top of the page and is one of the most important sections in terms of user navigation. It provides a space to introduce your website's identity, and it typically includes:

- **Logo**: Represents your brand or website. It's often linked to the homepage for easy navigation.
- **Title/Tagline**: Describes the purpose or name of the website.
- **Navigation Menu**: Includes links to different sections of the website, such as "Home," "About," "Services," "Contact," etc.

The header should be clean and concise to ensure users can quickly understand the website's purpose and navigate it easily.

b. Navigation

The **navigation** section allows users to explore different sections of the website. A good navigation system improves usability and makes it easier for visitors to find what they're looking for. Navigation can be placed in:

- **Top Navigation Bar**: Usually located at the top of the page, with horizontal links to the main sections of the site.
- **Side Navigation**: This vertical menu often appears on the left or right side of the page and can house subcategories or additional links.
- **Sticky Navigation**: Sometimes, the navigation bar can remain fixed at the top of the page while users scroll. This makes it accessible at all times.

Good navigation should be clear, intuitive, and consistent throughout the site.

c. Content Section

The **content section** is the heart of your page. This is where the main information of the page is displayed, whether it's text, images, videos, or any other type of content. When designing the content area, consider:

- **Organization**: Break the content into digestible sections, using headings, subheadings, paragraphs, and lists.
- **Multimedia**: Decide where images, videos, or other media should be placed to support the text.
- **Call-to-Action**: If your site is a business or service website, consider adding a clear call-to-action (CTA) button, such as "Contact Us," "Buy Now," or "Learn More."

It's crucial that the content area is well-organized and visually appealing to keep visitors engaged.

d. Footer

The **footer** is usually placed at the bottom of the page and typically contains secondary information that users may need, such as:

- **Copyright Information**: Often includes the copyright symbol and year.
- **Additional Links**: These could include privacy policy, terms of service, site map, or external links like social media icons.
- **Contact Info**: If not in the header or a dedicated section, your footer may contain contact information or a form.

While the footer is less important than the header or content section, it provides useful information without cluttering the primary sections of the page.

4. Moving from Wireframe to Implementation

Once you have your wireframe and layout plan in place, the next step in the web development process is the **implementation** phase. This involves translating the wireframe into actual code, using **HTML**, **CSS**, and **JavaScript** to bring the design to life. Let's break down each part of the implementation process:

---

1. HTML (Structure)

HTML (HyperText Markup Language) provides the basic structure of your web page. It defines the elements on your page, such as headings, paragraphs, navigation links, and multimedia. This is where you build the skeletal structure of your layout as per the wireframe.

Steps for Writing HTML:

- **Header**: Start by defining the header section. Typically, it contains the logo or website title, and the navigation bar.
- **Main Content Area**: This section will contain the primary content of the page, which could include articles, images, forms, and more.
- **Footer**: The footer usually contains copyright information, contact details, or links to privacy policies, etc.

Example HTML Structure:

Here's an example HTML layout that corresponds to the wireframe:

```
<!DOCTYPE html>
<html lang="en">
<head>
  <meta charset="UTF-8">
  <meta name="viewport" content="width=device-width, initial-scale=1.0">
  <title>My Website</title>
  <link rel="stylesheet" href="styles.css">
</head>
<body>
  <header>
    <h1>Website Title</h1>
    <nav>
      <ul>
        <li><a href="#">Home</a></li>
        <li><a href="#">About</a></li>
        <li><a href="#">Contact</a></li>
      </ul>
    </nav>
  </header>

  <main>
    <section>
```

```
    <h2>Welcome</h2>
    <p>This is the content area where you'll place your main content.</p>
    </section>
  </main>

  <footer>
    <p>&copy; 2025 My Website</p>
  </footer>
</body>
</html>
```

Explanation:

- **Header**: The header section includes the main title and a navigation menu. The `<nav>` element is used to contain the navigation links.
- **Main**: This contains the core content of your page. Here, we have a section with a heading and a paragraph. You can expand this section to include additional content like images, videos, or other components.
- **Footer**: The footer provides the site's copyright information and any additional links or details.

---

2. CSS (Styling)

Once the HTML structure is in place, the next step is to style the page using **CSS (Cascading Style Sheets)**. CSS allows you to control the visual appearance of your HTML elements, such as their color, layout, size, and positioning.

Steps for Writing CSS:

- **General Styling**: Start by styling elements like the header, footer, and main content area.
- **Layout**: Use CSS layout techniques such as Flexbox or Grid to create a responsive design that adapts to different screen sizes (for example, mobile, tablet, and desktop).
- **Colors and Fonts**: Define the color scheme and typography, including font families, sizes, and weights.

Example CSS:

Here's an example of CSS that complements the HTML structure above:

```
/* Reset some default browser styles */
* {
  margin: 0;
  padding: 0;
  box-sizing: border-box;
}

/* Body and overall layout */
body {
  font-family: Arial, sans-serif;
  line-height: 1.6;
```

```css
  background-color: #f4f4f4;
}

/* Header Styling */
header {
  background-color: #333;
  color: white;
  padding: 10px;
  text-align: center;
}

header h1 {
  font-size: 2rem;
}

/* Navigation Styling */
nav ul {
  list-style-type: none;
  padding: 0;
  text-align: center;
}

nav ul li {
  display: inline;
  margin-right: 20px;
}

nav ul li a {
  color: white;
  text-decoration: none;
}

nav ul li a:hover {
  text-decoration: underline;
}

/* Main Content Styling */
main {
  padding: 20px;
  background-color: white;
  margin: 20px auto;
  max-width: 900px;
}

section {
  margin-bottom: 20px;
}

h2 {
  color: #333;
  font-size: 1.5rem;
}

/* Footer Styling */
footer {
  background-color: #333;
  color: white;
```

```
    text-align: center;
    padding: 10px;
    position: relative;
    bottom: 0;
    width: 100%;
}
```
Explanation:

- **Reset Styles**: The * selector resets margin, padding, and box-sizing for all elements, ensuring consistent spacing across different browsers.
- **Body**: Set a standard font family and line height for readability, with a soft background color (#f4f4f4) for the whole page.
- **Header**: The header has a dark background with white text. The text is centered, and padding is added for spacing.
- **Navigation**: The navigation links are styled to display inline with some spacing between them. On hover, the links are underlined to provide interactivity feedback.
- **Main Content**: The main content area is centered on the page, with a maximum width of 900px for better readability on larger screens.
- **Footer**: The footer has similar styling to the header, ensuring consistency. It stays at the bottom of the page.

3. JavaScript (Interactivity)

JavaScript adds interactivity to your web page. This could involve simple actions like handling form submissions, adding dynamic elements such as a slider, or making your page more interactive by updating content dynamically.

Steps for Writing JavaScript:

- **DOM Manipulation**: You'll likely need JavaScript to interact with and modify HTML elements based on user interactions.
- **Event Handling**: Add event listeners to buttons, links, forms, and other elements to trigger actions like showing a message or submitting data.
- **Dynamic Changes**: Use JavaScript to change content, styles, or other aspects of the page based on user actions.

Example JavaScript:

Here's a simple example of JavaScript to show a message when a button is clicked:

```
document.addEventListener("DOMContentLoaded", function() {
  // Add event listener to the button
  const button = document.querySelector("button");

  button.addEventListener("click", function() {
    alert("Button clicked!");
```

```
  });
});
```
Explanation:

- **DOMContentLoaded**: This event ensures that the JavaScript code runs only after the HTML has been fully loaded.
- **Query Selector**: `document.querySelector("button")` selects the first button element on the page.
- **Event Listener**: The `click` event listener waits for the user to click the button, and when clicked, the `alert` function is called to display a message.

2. Combining HTML, XHTML, DHTML, and JavaScript

Web development relies on a variety of technologies to structure, style, and add interactivity to a page. **HTML, XHTML, DHTML**, and **JavaScript** each serve distinct roles in building a web page. Let's explore how these technologies work together to create a dynamic and functional user experience.

1. HTML (HyperText Markup Language)

HTML is the fundamental building block of any web page. It provides the structure and content by using a series of markup elements (tags). HTML defines the elements on the page such as headings, paragraphs, images, links, tables, forms, and more. Without HTML, there is no web page, as it lays the foundation for all content.

HTML Example:
```
<!DOCTYPE html>
<html lang="en">
<head>
  <meta charset="UTF-8">
  <meta name="viewport" content="width=device-width, initial-scale=1.0">
  <title>My Web Page</title>
</head>
<body>
  <header>
    <h1>Welcome to My Web Page</h1>
  </header>
  <section>
    <p>This is a paragraph of text.</p>
  </section>
  <footer>
    <p>© 2025 My Web Page</p>
  </footer>
</body>
</html>
```

- **Structure**: Elements like `<header>`, `<section>`, and `<footer>` are used to organize the content of the page.
- **Tags**: `<h1>` is used for headings, and `<p>` is used for paragraphs, defining the content and organization.

---

2. XHTML (Extensible HyperText Markup Language)

XHTML is a stricter version of HTML. While HTML is more flexible, XHTML follows XML (Extensible Markup Language) rules, which enforce stricter syntax and ensure that tags are properly nested and closed. XHTML makes it easier to maintain consistency in code, but it is less commonly used today because of modern HTML5 standards.

Key Differences Between HTML and XHTML:

- XHTML requires all tags to be properly closed, even self-closing ones, such as `<img />` or `<br />`.
- HTML allows certain flexibility with tag nesting and missing closing tags, but XHTML does not.

XHTML Example:
```
<!DOCTYPE html>
<html xmlns="http://www.w3.org/1999/xhtml">
<head>
  <meta charset="UTF-8" />
  <title>XHTML Example</title>
</head>
<body>
  <p>This is an XHTML compliant paragraph.</p>
</body>
</html>
```

- **Properly Closed Tags**: Notice that the self-closing `<meta />` tag in XHTML needs to have a slash before the closing angle bracket.
- **Strict Syntax**: All elements must be properly nested and closed, ensuring that the document adheres to XML rules.

---

3. DHTML (Dynamic HTML)

DHTML is not a new language but rather a combination of **HTML**, **CSS**, and **JavaScript** that allows you to create dynamic and interactive content. With DHTML, you can modify the HTML structure, CSS styles, and page elements dynamically without needing to reload the page.

- **HTML** provides the structure.
- **CSS** controls the layout and appearance.

- **JavaScript** enables the interactivity, handling dynamic changes on the page in response to user actions.

Example of DHTML in Action:

Imagine you want to change the color of a div when a user clicks a button. Here's how you can use JavaScript (as part of DHTML) to dynamically modify the page:

```html
<!DOCTYPE html>
<html lang="en">
<head>
  <meta charset="UTF-8">
  <title>DHTML Example</title>
  <style>
    #myDiv {
      width: 200px;
      height: 100px;
      background-color: blue;
    }
  </style>
  <script>
    function changeColor() {
      document.getElementById("myDiv").style.backgroundColor = "red";
    }
  </script>
</head>
<body>
  <button onclick="changeColor()">Click to Change Color</button>
  <div id="myDiv"></div>
</body>
</html>
```

- **HTML**: Creates the structure of the page, including the button and the `div` element.
- **CSS**: Defines the initial appearance of the `div` (e.g., blue background color).
- **JavaScript**: Handles the interaction (changing the background color of the `div` to red when the button is clicked).

This is a basic example of how **DHTML** works to create dynamic, real-time changes on a web page without needing to reload or navigate away from the page.

4. JavaScript (Interactivity and Behavior)

JavaScript is a dynamic, high-level scripting language that adds interactivity to web pages. It is responsible for responding to user actions like clicks, form submissions, and mouse movements. It can also modify HTML elements, change the page structure, and control the browser's behavior.

JavaScript is critical for creating interactive web pages. It can:

- Handle user input (form validation, button clicks).
- Update the content of the page (dynamic content changes without reloading the page).
- Provide real-time feedback (alerts, pop-ups).
- Interact with external resources (fetch data, AJAX requests).

JavaScript Example:

Here's a simple example where JavaScript is used to show an alert when a button is clicked:

```
<button onclick="alert('Hello, World!')">Click Me!</button>
```

- When the user clicks the button, JavaScript triggers the `alert()` function, which displays a popup with the message `"Hello, World!"`.

How These Technologies Work Together

- **HTML** forms the structure of your web page.
- **XHTML** ensures that your HTML is strict and follows the rules of XML (but HTML5 is now more commonly used, offering flexibility with some of the stricter rules of XHTML).
- **DHTML** combines HTML, CSS, and JavaScript to allow for dynamic, interactive elements that don't require page reloads.
- **JavaScript** adds the behavior and interactivity to the page, making it more user-friendly and responsive.

When used together, these technologies create a seamless user experience. HTML structures the content, CSS controls the look and layout, JavaScript brings interactivity, and DHTML combines them all to create a dynamic, real-time web experience.

3. Creating a Responsive Web Design

A responsive web design ensures that your website looks good on all devices (desktops, tablets, smartphones). This is achieved by using flexible grids, images, and media queries in CSS.

- **Flexible Layout**: Use percentages instead of fixed pixel values to create a fluid layout. For example, instead of setting a fixed width of 600px, you can use:

```
.container {
  width: 80%;  /* 80% of the viewport width */
}
```

- **Media Queries**: Media queries allow you to apply different styles based on the device's screen size. For example:

```
@media (max-width: 600px) {
  .container {
    width: 100%;
  }
}
```

This ensures that when the screen width is 600px or less (i.e., on mobile devices), the container's width will be set to 100%.

- **Responsive Images**: Use the `srcset` attribute in `<img>` tags to serve different images based on the device's screen resolution and size. For example:

```
<img src="image.jpg" srcset="image-small.jpg 500w, image-large.jpg 1000w" alt="Example image">
```

A responsive design adapts the page layout and content for any screen size, ensuring that the user experience remains optimal.

---

4. Testing and Debugging Your Code

Testing and debugging are essential steps in the web development process. They ensure that your code is working as expected, user interactions are smooth, and no errors hinder the user experience. Below is a more detailed explanation of the various aspects of testing and debugging a web page:

---

1. Browser Testing

Web pages may look and behave differently across various browsers due to discrepancies in how each browser interprets HTML, CSS, and JavaScript. **Browser testing** is the process of verifying that your website functions properly on different browsers.

Why Browser Testing Is Important:

- **Browser Compatibility:** Different browsers may have different support for HTML and CSS standards, and JavaScript engines can vary.
- **Rendering Differences:** Each browser may render the page slightly differently in terms of layout and design.
- **Functionality Issues:** Some JavaScript features might not be supported or could behave differently on older versions of browsers.

1. **Manual Testing**: Open your webpage in different browsers (e.g., Chrome, Firefox, Safari, Microsoft Edge) to verify how it appears and functions.
2. **Automated Testing Tools**: Use online tools like **BrowserStack** or **Sauce Labs** to automate the testing across different browser versions and operating systems.
3. **Cross-browser Compatibility**: Ensure that essential features such as navigation, buttons, and forms work seamlessly across all major browsers.

---

2. Responsive Testing

With the increasing use of mobile devices, it's important to ensure your web page is **responsive**. **Responsive design** allows your webpage to adapt to different screen sizes and devices (such as smartphones, tablets, and desktops).

Why Responsive Testing Is Important:

- **Mobile-first Experience**: A large portion of users may access your website from mobile devices, and a responsive layout ensures they have a good experience.
- **Screen Size Variability**: Devices come in a variety of screen sizes, so your design needs to adapt to these sizes seamlessly.
- **Usability and Accessibility**: A responsive design improves readability, navigation, and overall usability across devices.

How to Perform Responsive Testing:

1. **Device Simulation in Developer Tools**: Modern browsers have developer tools (like Chrome DevTools) that allow you to simulate different device screen sizes and resolutions.
   - In **Chrome**: Open DevTools (Ctrl+Shift+I or F12), then click on the device toolbar (Ctrl+Shift+M). You can choose different devices like mobile phones and tablets or enter custom screen sizes.

   Example:

   ```
   // Check how the layout behaves for a mobile screen:
   console.log('Switching to mobile view');
   ```

2. **Testing on Real Devices**: While browser tools can simulate devices, testing on actual devices gives the best insight into the behavior of your page on mobile and tablet devices.
3. **Using Responsiveness CSS Techniques**: Make sure your CSS uses techniques such as **media queries** to adjust the layout based on the screen size. For example:

   ```
   @media (max-width: 768px) {
     /* Mobile-specific styles */
   ```

```
  body {
    font-size: 14px;
  }
}
```

4. **Tools for Automated Testing**: You can use tools like **Google Lighthouse** to test your site's performance, accessibility, and responsiveness.

---

3. Debugging with Console

Debugging is the process of identifying and fixing issues in your code. The **console** is a powerful tool in the browser's developer tools that helps developers track issues, output values, and inspect code execution flow.

Why the Console Is Useful:

- **Logging Information**: Helps log data or messages to check the flow of code and identify issues.
- **Tracking Variables**: You can log the values of variables and see how they change during execution.
- **Identifying Errors**: Errors like JavaScript exceptions or syntax issues are shown in the console, helping you pinpoint where the code breaks.

How to Use the Console:

1. **Logging Messages and Variables**: The `console.log()` function is commonly used to log messages and data in the browser console.

   ```
   let username = "Alice";
   console.log("Current username: " + username);
   ```

2. **Inspecting Errors**: The console will also show errors if JavaScript code fails (e.g., syntax errors or runtime errors). These messages can help you understand what went wrong.

   ```
   // Example of error message in console:
   Uncaught ReferenceError: someVariable is not defined
   ```

3. **Using Console for Debugging**: Set breakpoints, track variables, and step through your code to identify issues in the flow.
   - To debug in **Chrome DevTools**: Go to the **Sources** tab, find the script, and click the line number to add a breakpoint. Then, when the page is refreshed, the debugger will pause at that line.
4. **Other Console Methods**: You can also use other console methods for debugging:
   - `console.error()` for errors
   - `console.warn()` for warnings
   - `console.table()` for structured data visualization (e.g., arrays, objects)

4. Fixing Common Issues

As you test and debug your code, you will likely encounter several common issues. These issues can typically be fixed by following a systematic approach:

Common Issues in Web Development:

1. **Unclosed HTML Tags**: Always make sure that your HTML tags are properly opened and closed. Unclosed tags can cause rendering issues.

   Example:

   ```
   <div>
     <p>This paragraph is inside a div.</p>
   </div> <!-- Don't forget to close your tags! -->
   ```

2. **CSS Selector Issues**: If elements are not styled as expected, check the CSS selectors for accuracy. Ensure they match the correct HTML elements.

   Example:

   ```
   /* Correct selector */
   #header {
     font-size: 20px;
   }

   /* Potential issue if the selector doesn't match the HTML element */
   .header {  /* Might not work if the id is used in the HTML */
     font-size: 20px;
   }
   ```

3. **JavaScript Errors**: Syntax or runtime errors can break your code, especially when manipulating the DOM or handling events. Check the **Console** for error messages and use the `console.log()` method to troubleshoot.
4. **Broken Links or Images**: Ensure that all links (`<a>` tags) and images (`<img>` tags) are correct and point to the correct resources.
   o Check the paths (absolute or relative) and make sure files are located where the code expects them to be.
5. **Cross-Browser Compatibility**: As discussed earlier, test your page in different browsers and ensure that everything is displayed and functions correctly. Consider using CSS prefixes for compatibility and writing JavaScript code that works across all browsers.
6. **Form Validation**: Make sure that your forms are correctly validated before submission. JavaScript can be used to ensure users input the correct data format (e.g., email, phone numbers).

5. General Debugging Best Practices

Debugging is an essential part of the web development process. It allows you to identify and resolve issues that may arise during the development of a web page or application. Adopting best practices for debugging will help make this process more efficient and effective. Here are some of the most widely recommended debugging practices:

---

1. Start Simple

When beginning the debugging process, it's essential to **start with small chunks of code** rather than jumping into complex sections of the codebase. This helps isolate the issue more quickly and avoid overwhelming yourself with unnecessary details.

Why Start Simple?

- **Isolate the Problem**: By breaking down the code into smaller parts, you can more easily pinpoint where things go wrong.
- **Eliminate Unnecessary Complexity**: Debugging a large block of code can be confusing and make it difficult to see the actual issue. Starting small keeps things manageable.
- **Faster Debugging**: If you start with a simpler version of your code and verify that it works, you can gradually introduce complexity, verifying functionality as you go.

How to Start Simple:

- Write basic code snippets and test them first before adding complexity.
- Use **console.log()** to output values and ensure each part of your code is functioning correctly.
- Build the core functionality first, and only introduce features that build upon the basic functionality once the core works as expected.

Example:

```
// Start simple: Testing a basic function first
function add(a, b) {
  console.log(a + b); // Log to check
}
add(1, 2);  // Output: 3
```

After ensuring that the basic function works, you can incrementally add more features, like user input validation or dynamic functionality, testing along the way.

---

2. Check Browser Console Regularly

The **browser console** is one of the most valuable tools for debugging JavaScript. It's important to keep an eye on the console, as it will often provide error messages, logs, warnings, and insights into your code's execution flow.

Why the Browser Console Is Crucial:

- **Error Reporting**: The console displays detailed error messages, including line numbers, which can help you identify where the problem is located.
- **Real-Time Debugging**: It provides real-time feedback on JavaScript code execution, allowing you to track issues as they happen.
- **Logging Variables and Functions**: `console.log()`, `console.warn()`, and `console.error()` can be used to output variable values, function results, and trace errors in your code.

Best Practices for Using the Browser Console:

- **Log Critical Data**: Use `console.log()` to output values, function results, or errors that might give clues about what's wrong.

  ```
  console.log("The value of x is:", x);
  console.error("This is an error message.");
  ```

- **Inspect Errors**: The console typically displays stack traces for errors, showing where in the code the error occurred. Inspecting these will direct you to the root cause.
- **Filter Logs**: Modern browsers allow you to filter logs based on types (e.g., logs, warnings, errors), which helps focus on relevant information.

---

3. Use Developer Tools

All major browsers (Chrome, Firefox, Edge, Safari) come with **developer tools** that provide a powerful suite of tools for inspecting, debugging, and optimizing your web page.

Why Developer Tools Are Essential:

- **Inspect Elements**: You can examine the HTML structure and CSS styles applied to elements in real-time, helping you debug layout issues.
- **Network Requests**: Check whether your network requests (API calls, image loading, etc.) are succeeding or failing. This is essential when working with external data or services.
- **JavaScript Debugging**: The **Sources** tab in developer tools allows you to set breakpoints, step through code, and inspect variables, making it easier to track down runtime issues.
- **Performance Monitoring**: Track memory usage, page load times, and more to optimize the performance of your site.

How to Use Developer Tools:

- **Open Developer Tools**: In most browsers, press `F12` or `Ctrl+Shift+I` to open Developer Tools.
- **Inspect HTML/CSS**: Use the **Elements** tab to inspect and edit the HTML and CSS of your page in real-time.
- **Debug JavaScript**: Use the **Sources** tab to step through JavaScript code using breakpoints and inspect the call stack.
- **Network Analysis**: Use the **Network** tab to monitor requests and responses between your page and the server.

Example (in Chrome Developer Tools):

- **Inspecting a Button**: Right-click a button and select "Inspect" to view its HTML structure and CSS rules applied.
- **Setting a Breakpoint**: In the **Sources** tab, find your script and click the line number to set a breakpoint. The code will pause at that line, allowing you to step through it.

---

4. Automated Testing

Automated testing helps catch errors early and ensures that your code works as expected without the need for manual testing every time you make changes.

Why Automated Testing Is Important:

- **Catch Errors Early**: Automated tests can catch errors during development, preventing bugs from making it into production.
- **Save Time**: Once you set up automated tests, you don't have to manually test every change you make to the codebase.
- **Ensure Stability**: Automated tests help ensure that new code doesn't break existing functionality (regression testing).
- **Test Complex Scenarios**: Automated testing can handle repetitive tasks or complex edge cases more efficiently than manual testing.

Popular Testing Tools:

- **Jest**: A JavaScript testing framework that allows you to write unit tests and integrate them with your development workflow.
- **Selenium**: A tool for automating web browsers to simulate user interactions and test web applications.
- **Cypress**: A testing framework designed for end-to-end testing of modern web applications.
- **Mocha**: Another popular testing framework for JavaScript, often used in combination with Chai for assertions.

Example (using Jest):

```
// Test a simple function
function add(a, b) {
  return a + b;
}

test('adds 1 + 2 to equal 3', () => {
  expect(add(1, 2)).toBe(3);
});
```

Automated tests run regularly (especially after each code change) and provide feedback on the quality of your code.

---

5. Test in Multiple Environments

Testing your website across various environments is a crucial step in ensuring that it works properly for all users, regardless of the browser, device, or operating system they are using. Testing in different environments helps identify and fix issues related to **cross-browser compatibility**, **different screen sizes**, and **operating system differences**.

Let's dive into the importance and methods for testing in multiple environments.

Why Testing in Multiple Environments Is Crucial

1. Cross-Browser Compatibility

Different web browsers, such as **Google Chrome**, **Mozilla Firefox**, **Microsoft Edge**, **Safari**, and **Internet Explorer**, have slight variations in how they interpret **HTML**, **CSS**, and **JavaScript**. These differences can cause issues, such as layout discrepancies, broken JavaScript functionality, or CSS that doesn't render properly.

For example, **CSS Flexbox** might work seamlessly in Chrome but cause issues in older versions of Internet Explorer. Additionally, JavaScript features like **async/await** or **fetch()** may not be fully supported in older browser versions.

Testing across multiple browsers ensures that your website functions correctly for users on all browsers.

2. Different Screen Sizes and Devices

Websites must be **responsive**, meaning they should adapt to different screen sizes and devices. Mobile users, tablet users, and desktop users all interact with your site in different ways. Testing your website on various devices ensures that it **looks good** and is **usable** across all screen sizes.

- **Desktop**: Larger screens often have more real estate for content, and interactions may rely on a mouse.
- **Mobile**: Smaller screens require a mobile-friendly design, and users rely on touch interactions.
- **Tablet**: Tablets are in-between mobile and desktop screens, with a mix of touch and mouse interactions.

Without testing your design for all these different screen sizes, you risk providing a poor user experience, where elements might overflow, break, or not display properly.

3. Operating System Differences

Browsers behave differently on **Windows**, **macOS**, and **Linux**. Even within the same browser, rendering might differ across operating systems. For example, fonts may look different, the appearance of UI elements (like buttons) may vary, and some JavaScript functions may have platform-specific behaviors.

Testing across operating systems ensures that your website delivers a consistent experience, regardless of the platform your users are on.

How to Test in Multiple Environments

1. Use Browser-Specific Tools

Most modern browsers come with built-in tools to help simulate various devices and screen sizes for testing. These tools allow you to view your site in **different device configurations** without needing the actual devices.

For example:

- **Google Chrome**: Chrome's **DevTools** provides a **Device Mode** where you can simulate a wide range of mobile devices. This includes options to adjust screen size, resolution, and even simulate network conditions.

  To enable Device Mode in Chrome:

    o Open Chrome DevTools (F12 or Ctrl+Shift+I).
    o Click the **Toggle Device Toolbar** icon (a small phone and tablet).
    o Select from a list of devices or enter custom screen sizes.

- **Firefox**: Firefox also offers similar features through its **Responsive Design Mode**, accessible from the DevTools panel. You can simulate various devices and screen sizes directly within the browser.

2. Cross-Browser Testing Services

Testing on real devices and across browsers can be time-consuming and expensive. Instead, you can use **cross-browser testing services** like **BrowserStack** or **Sauce Labs**. These platforms let you test your website on **virtualized** or **real devices** running multiple operating systems and browsers.

With these services, you can:

- Test your site on different browsers (e.g., Chrome, Firefox, Safari, Edge) across **multiple versions**.
- Access a wide range of devices (iPhone, Android, tablets, etc.).
- Perform automated tests and screenshots to ensure consistency across browsers and devices.

Example:

- BrowserStack allows you to select a browser version, operating system (Windows, macOS, Linux), and device to test your website without needing to install or maintain multiple devices and browsers.

3. Responsive Testing

In addition to simulating devices in browsers, it's important to test how your website adapts to various screen sizes. **Responsive web design** ensures that your website layout and content adjust automatically based on the screen size and device type.

- **Chrome DevTools**: As mentioned earlier, the **Device Mode** in Chrome's DevTools is great for testing responsiveness. It simulates mobile devices, tablets, and desktops, showing how your site behaves on different resolutions.
- **Firefox Responsive Design Mode**: Similar to Chrome, Firefox's developer tools offer a **Responsive Design Mode** that enables testing across different device resolutions.
- **Manual Testing**: In addition to using browser tools, it's always beneficial to manually check the responsiveness by resizing your browser window on different devices to ensure the layout adjusts as expected.

Example Code:

Here's a simple example of how you can use **CSS media queries** to make a webpage responsive:

```
/* Default styles for large screens */
body {
  font-size: 16px;
}
```

```
/* Smaller screens like tablets */
@media (max-width: 768px) {
  body {
    font-size: 14px;
  }
}

/* Very small screens like mobile */
@media (max-width: 480px) {
  body {
    font-size: 12px;
  }
}
```

Example: Simulating Mobile View in Chrome DevTools

To test your site for mobile responsiveness, you can use **Chrome DevTools** to simulate how the page will look on a mobile device:

1. Open Chrome DevTools (`F12` or `Ctrl+Shift+I`).
2. Click the **Device Toolbar** icon (top-left corner).
3. Select a device from the drop-down menu (e.g., iPhone X, Galaxy S5, etc.).
4. Your page will now simulate the mobile device's screen size, and you can interact with it as though you are using that device.

```
// Example JavaScript: Simulating mobile view for testing purposes
console.log('Testing layout in mobile view');
```

In the example above, you can use `console.log()` to help track when and where you're testing specific parts of your layout, ensuring that you debug effectively during this phase.

5. Publishing Your Web Page Online

Once you've completed the development, testing, and debugging of your web page, the next critical step is publishing it online so that others can access it. This process involves several steps, including choosing a **web hosting provider**, registering a **domain name**, uploading your files to the server, and ensuring your site is secure. Here's a detailed explanation of each step:

1. Web Hosting

Web hosting refers to the service that allows you to store your website's files and make them accessible on the internet. Hosting providers offer different types of services, ranging from free plans (for static websites) to paid services (for more complex websites with additional features).

Options for Hosting:

- **Free Hosting Providers**:
  - ○ **GitHub Pages**: A free service for hosting static websites directly from a GitHub repository. This is ideal for personal projects, portfolios, blogs, or small websites.
    - ▪ **Steps to publish on GitHub Pages**:
      1. Create a GitHub repository and push your website files (HTML, CSS, JavaScript).
      2. In the repository settings, scroll down to the **GitHub Pages** section.
      3. Select the branch (e.g., `main`) to publish, and GitHub will serve the site for you.
      4. Your website will be available at `https://username.github.io/repository-name`.
  - ○ **Netlify**: Offers free hosting with features like continuous deployment, custom domains, and SSL encryption. You can connect it directly to your Git repository (e.g., GitHub, GitLab).
    - ▪ **Steps to publish on Netlify**:
      1. Connect your GitHub account to Netlify.
      2. Select the repository containing your site.
      3. Netlify will automatically deploy and generate a live URL.
      4. You can configure a custom domain for your site.
- **Paid Hosting Providers**:
  - ○ **Bluehost, HostGator, SiteGround**, and others offer various hosting plans with additional features like:
    - ▪ **Custom domain names** (e.g., www.yoursite.com)
    - ▪ **SSL certificates** (secure HTTPS connections)
    - ▪ **Database support** (for dynamic websites with backend databases)
    - ▪ **Email hosting** (create custom email addresses like info@yoursite.com)
    - ▪ **Higher performance and reliability** (faster load times, uptime guarantees)

These services are ideal for more complex websites, e-commerce stores, or projects requiring specific server-side functionalities.

Choosing a Hosting Provider:

When choosing a hosting provider, consider the following:

- **Website requirements** (static vs. dynamic site, traffic expectations)
- **Budget** (free hosting for simple sites vs. paid hosting for more features)
- **Support** (customer service and documentation)
- **Scalability** (whether the hosting can handle growing traffic over time)

2. Domain Name

A **domain name** is your website's unique address on the internet (e.g., `www.example.com`). Without a domain, your site would have to rely on an IP address, which is not user-friendly.

How to Buy a Domain Name:

- You can purchase a domain name from domain registrars such as **GoDaddy**, **Namecheap**, or **Google Domains**.
- When purchasing a domain, ensure it is easy to remember, relevant to your website's content, and, if possible, short and simple.

Steps to purchase and configure a domain:

1. **Search for Availability**: Use a domain registrar to search for an available name. For example, go to GoDaddy and search for the domain you want to register.
2. **Purchase**: After finding an available domain, add it to your cart and complete the checkout process.
3. **DNS Configuration**: Once you've purchased the domain, configure its **DNS settings** (Domain Name System) to point to your hosting provider. This typically involves adding **A records** or **CNAME records** to connect your domain to your hosting server.

---

3. Uploading Files

Once you've chosen a hosting provider and set up your domain name, the next step is to upload your files (HTML, CSS, JavaScript, images) to the server so that users can access them.

File Upload Methods:

- **FTP (File Transfer Protocol)**: You can use an **FTP client** like **FileZilla** to upload your website files to your hosting server. This method requires:
    - FTP server details (provided by your hosting service, including the server address, username, and password).
    - Using FTP software, connect to the server and transfer your local files to the correct folder (usually `public_html` or `www`).
- **Hosting Dashboard**: Many hosting providers offer a **web-based file manager** that allows you to upload files directly from the dashboard without needing an FTP client.

Steps to upload using FTP:

1. Download and install an FTP client like **FileZilla**.
2. Connect to your hosting server by entering the FTP credentials provided by your hosting provider.
3. Drag and drop your website files into the correct directory on the server (e.g., `public_html`).

4. Once the files are uploaded, visit your website's domain to see the live version.

4. SSL Certification

An **SSL certificate** (Secure Socket Layer) encrypts data between the user's browser and your web server. It ensures that sensitive data, such as passwords or credit card information, is protected from interception by third parties.

Why SSL is Important:

- **Security**: It encrypts the connection between the server and the user's browser, ensuring any transmitted data is protected.
- **SEO benefits**: Search engines like Google prefer secure sites and give them a ranking boost.
- **User trust**: Websites with SSL certificates are marked with a **green padlock** symbol in browsers, signaling to users that the site is secure.

Getting SSL:

- **Free SSL**: Some hosting providers (like **Netlify**, **GitHub Pages**, or **Cloudflare**) offer **free SSL certificates** via **Let's Encrypt**.
- **Paid SSL**: Paid hosting services often provide SSL certificates as part of their plans. Alternatively, you can purchase an SSL certificate from providers like **Comodo** or **GlobalSign**.

Steps to install SSL:

1. If using a free service like **Let's Encrypt**, follow the instructions to generate and install the certificate.
2. On paid hosting services, SSL installation might be automatic, or you may need to request and install the certificate from the hosting control panel.
3. After installation, your website will load using **HTTPS** (instead of HTTP).

5. Final Testing and Launch

Before launching your site, conduct final tests:

- **Check all links** to ensure they are working.
- **Test the forms** (e.g., contact forms) to ensure data is being submitted correctly.
- **Ensure SSL** is active and the website is served via HTTPS.
- **Verify responsiveness** on mobile, tablet, and desktop devices.
- **Cross-browser testing** to check compatibility across different browsers.

Once you've confirmed everything works, your website is ready to go live!

Summary

Building your first web page is a combination of planning, designing, and technical implementation. Here's a recap of the steps:

1. **Planning Layout**: Understand your content and design layout using wireframes.
2. **Combining Technologies**: Use HTML for structure, CSS for style, JavaScript for interactivity, and optional XHTML/DHTML for stricter syntax and dynamic content.
3. **Responsive Design**: Use CSS and media queries to ensure your site works well on all devices.
4. **Testing and Debugging**: Test across browsers and devices, and debug using browser tools.
5. **Publishing**: Host your site on a web server and ensure it's accessible via a domain name.

By following these steps, you can create a web page that not only functions well but also looks great across various devices and platforms.

CHAPTER 7: BEST PRACTICES AND WEB DEVELOPMENT TIPS

1. Clean Code and Commenting

Writing **clean code** is one of the most important aspects of software development. Clean code is easy to read, understand, and maintain. It reduces complexity and makes collaboration with other developers more efficient.

Key Principles of Clean Code:

- **Meaningful Variable and Function Names**: Choose descriptive names for variables, functions, and classes. Avoid using vague or cryptic names like a, b, or temp. For example, use totalPrice instead of just price if it represents the final price after discounts.
- **Avoid Redundancy**: Don't repeat the same logic in multiple places. Instead, use functions, loops, or classes to handle repeated actions.
- **Keep Functions Small and Focused**: A function should do one thing and do it well. If a function is doing too many things, it becomes difficult to understand and maintain.
- **Use Consistent Formatting**: Stick to a uniform coding style, including indentation, spacing, and line breaks. This makes your code more readable to others.
- **Error Handling**: Proper error handling is a hallmark of clean code. Make sure errors are caught and handled appropriately to avoid unexpected issues.

Commenting Code:

While clean code is self-explanatory, comments are still essential for providing context, explaining why certain decisions were made, and guiding future developers.

- **Use Comments to Explain Why, Not What**: The code itself should tell the "what," but the "why" often requires a comment. For example, if you're using a specific algorithm for performance reasons, explain that in a comment.
- **Avoid Over-Commenting**: Don't comment every line of code. Comments should be used to clarify the logic or to explain complex or non-obvious code.
- **Use Block Comments for Larger Explanations**: For large chunks of logic or complex algorithms, use block comments.

Example of clean code with comments:

```
// Calculate the discount amount based on the total price
function calculateDiscount(totalPrice) {
    let discountRate = 0.1; // 10% discount
    return totalPrice * discountRate;
}
```

2. Accessibility and SEO (Search Engine Optimization) Basics

Accessibility (A11Y):

Making websites accessible means ensuring that users, regardless of their abilities, can interact with your site. This is important for people with disabilities, but it's also beneficial for a wider audience, such as those with poor internet connections or old devices.

- **Semantic HTML**: Use HTML elements according to their intended purpose (e.g., `<header>`, `<footer>`, `<article>`, `<section>`). This helps screen readers and other assistive devices understand the structure of the page.
- **Alt Text for Images**: Always include descriptive `alt` attributes for images to help visually impaired users who rely on screen readers.
- **Keyboard Navigation**: Ensure that your website is fully navigable using a keyboard, particularly for users who can't use a mouse. Use proper focus management (`tabindex`, `aria-*` attributes).
- **Color Contrast**: Make sure there's sufficient contrast between text and background colors to aid users with low vision or color blindness.

Example:

```
<img src="cat.jpg" alt="A cute cat sitting on a chair.">
```
SEO Basics:

SEO is the practice of optimizing your website to rank higher in search engine results, making it more discoverable.

- **Use Proper HTML Tags**: Make sure to use proper header tags (`<h1>`, `<h2>`, etc.) to structure your content. Search engines prioritize these tags to understand the main topics of your page.
- **Title and Meta Tags**: Always use descriptive and unique `<title>` and `<meta description>` tags. These help search engines understand the content of your page and improve click-through rates.
- **Alt Text for Images**: In addition to accessibility, alt text helps search engines index your images.
- **Linking**: Internal links (links to other pages within your site) and external links (links to other authoritative sites) improve SEO.
- **Mobile-Friendly Design**: Google prioritizes mobile-friendly sites in search results, so make sure your site is responsive.

Example of SEO-friendly code:

```
<head>
  <title>Best Cat Pictures</title>
  <meta name="description" content="A collection of the cutest cat pictures
from around the world.">
</head>
```

3. Mobile-Friendly Design and Responsive Layouts

In today's world, many users access websites through mobile devices, so it's important to design websites that adapt to different screen sizes and orientations.

Responsive Web Design (RWD):

Responsive design ensures your website looks good on all screen sizes (desktops, tablets, smartphones). The goal is to create one version of your site that works on any device, rather than having separate versions for different devices.

- **Fluid Grids**: Use percentage-based widths for elements rather than fixed widths in pixels. This ensures that the layout adapts to the screen size.
- **Media Queries**: CSS media queries allow you to apply styles based on the device's screen size, resolution, and orientation. You can define different rules for mobile, tablet, and desktop.

Example of a media query for mobile:

```
@media (max-width: 768px) {
    body {
        font-size: 14px;
    }
    header {
        padding: 10px;
    }
}
```

- **Flexible Images**: Ensure that images are responsive by setting their width to 100% and adjusting their height automatically.

Example:

```
img {
    max-width: 100%;
    height: auto;
}
```

- **Viewport Meta Tag**: This tag tells the browser how to scale and size the page on mobile devices.

Example:

```
<meta name="viewport" content="width=device-width, initial-scale=1">
```

4. Web Security Basics

Web security is crucial to protect both your website and its users from threats like hacking, phishing, and data breaches. Here are some key best practices:

Key Web Security Practices:

- **Use HTTPS (SSL/TLS)**: Ensure your website uses HTTPS instead of HTTP. This encrypts the data exchanged between the user and your site, protecting sensitive information like login credentials.
- **Input Validation**: Always validate and sanitize user input to prevent attacks like SQL injection or cross-site scripting (XSS).
- **Use Strong Passwords**: For any login or authentication system, ensure strong password policies and consider implementing multi-factor authentication (MFA).
- **Regular Software Updates**: Keep all server-side software, frameworks, libraries, and plugins up to date to protect against vulnerabilities.
- **Security Headers**: Implement security HTTP headers like `Content-Security-Policy`, `Strict-Transport-Security`, and `X-Content-Type-Options` to protect your website from various types of attacks.

Example of a secure header:

```
Strict-Transport-Security: max-age=31536000; includeSubDomains
```

5. Resources for Further Learning

As web development is constantly evolving, it's important to keep learning and improving your skills. Here are some excellent resources to help you stay up-to-date:

1. Documentation and References:

- **MDN Web Docs**: Mozilla's comprehensive documentation for HTML, CSS, JavaScript, and web APIs. (MDN Web Docs)
- **W3Schools**: A popular web development tutorial website that provides tutorials and references. (W3Schools)

2. Online Courses:

- **freeCodeCamp**: Offers free coding tutorials and certifications for HTML, CSS, JavaScript, and more. (freeCodeCamp)
- **Coursera**: Offers online courses from top universities and companies on web development topics. (Coursera)
- **Udemy**: A marketplace for online learning, with numerous web development courses. (Udemy)

3. Communities:

- **Stack Overflow**: A Q&A platform for developers where you can ask questions and share knowledge. (Stack Overflow)
- **Dev.to**: A community of developers sharing articles, tutorials, and discussions. (Dev.to)

4. Blogs and Tutorials:

- **CSS-Tricks**: A website filled with tutorials on CSS, JavaScript, and web design techniques. (<u>CSS-Tricks</u>)
- **Smashing Magazine**: A website providing web development, design tutorials, and industry news. (<u>Smashing Magazine</u>)

By leveraging these resources, you can stay current with the latest trends and techniques in web development.

APPENDICES

. Glossary of Web Development Terms

Understanding web development terminology is essential for effective communication and problem-solving when working on a website. Below are key terms related to web development:

HTML (HyperText Markup Language)

The standard language used to create web pages. It provides the structure of the web page using elements like headings, paragraphs, links, and images.

CSS (Cascading Style Sheets)

CSS is used to style and layout HTML elements, including changes to colors, fonts, spacing, and positioning.

JavaScript (JS)

A programming language that enables interactivity on web pages. It allows you to manipulate HTML and CSS elements dynamically.

XHTML (Extensible HyperText Markup Language)

An XML-based version of HTML, stricter in syntax rules. XHTML requires all tags to be properly closed and attributes to be quoted.

DHTML (Dynamic HTML)

A combination of HTML, CSS, and JavaScript used to create interactive and animated web pages that can change dynamically without reloading.

Responsive Design

A web design approach that ensures web pages look good on all devices (desktop, tablet, mobile) by adjusting layout and elements based on the device's screen size.

DOM (Document Object Model)

A programming interface for web documents. It represents the page as a tree structure where each node is an object representing part of the page, allowing JavaScript to manipulate the page dynamically.

API (Application Programming Interface)

A set of rules that allow different software programs to communicate with each other. In web development, APIs allow web pages to interact with external services (e.g., weather data or social media feeds).

AJAX (Asynchronous JavaScript and XML)

A technique that allows web pages to request data from a server and update parts of a page without reloading the whole page.

Bootstrap

A popular open-source CSS framework that provides pre-built components and responsive grid systems, helping developers create responsive and mobile-friendly web pages quickly.

SEO (Search Engine Optimization)

The process of improving the visibility of a website or webpage in search engine results pages (SERPs) through techniques such as keyword optimization, link-building, and content structuring.

JavaScript Framework

A pre-written collection of JavaScript code that makes it easier to develop interactive web applications. Examples include React, Angular, and Vue.js.

Version Control

The management of changes to source code over time, allowing developers to track and revert changes. Git is the most commonly used version control system.

Web Hosting

The service that stores and makes your website accessible over the internet. Providers offer various hosting types, such as shared, VPS, or dedicated hosting.

API Key

A unique identifier used to authenticate requests to an API. It acts like a password to access third-party services and ensure secure communication.

2. Common HTML, XHTML, and JavaScript Errors and How to Fix Them

HTML Errors:

1. **Unclosed Tags**:
   - **Error**: A tag is not properly closed (e.g., `<div>` without `</div>`).
   - **Fix**: Always ensure that all tags are properly closed, and nested tags are placed correctly.
   - **Example Fix**:

   ```
   <div>Content here</div> <!-- Correct -->
   <div>Content here <!-- Incorrect -->
   ```

2. **Invalid Attribute Values**:
   - **Error**: Incorrect attribute values, such as missing quotation marks.
   - **Fix**: Always use quotes around attribute values.
   - **Example Fix**:

   ```
   <img src="image.jpg" alt="Description"> <!-- Correct -->
   <img src=image.jpg alt=Description> <!-- Incorrect -->
   ```

3. **Missing DOCTYPE Declaration**:
   - **Error**: Forgetting to include `<!DOCTYPE html>` at the beginning of the HTML file.
   - **Fix**: Always include the DOCTYPE declaration to specify the document type.
   - **Example Fix**:

   ```
   <!DOCTYPE html> <!-- Correct -->
   ```

XHTML Errors:

1. **Unclosed Tags**:
   - **Error**: Tags must be properly closed in XHTML.
   - **Fix**: Ensure that tags are self-closed where needed (e.g., `<img />` or `<br />`).
   - **Example Fix**:

   ```
   <img src="image.jpg" alt="Image description" /> <!-- Correct for
   XHTML -->
   ```

2. **Case Sensitivity**:
   - **Error**: In XHTML, all tags and attributes must be lowercase.
   - **Fix**: Use lowercase for all tags and attributes.
   - **Example Fix**:

   ```
   <div>Content here</div> <!-- Correct for XHTML -->
   ```

JavaScript Errors:

1. **Syntax Errors**:
   - **Error**: Missing semicolon, unmatched parentheses, or brackets.
   - **Fix**: Carefully check the syntax, ensuring all code blocks are correctly closed.
   - **Example Fix**:

```
let x = 5; // Correct
let x = 5 // Incorrect
```

2. **Reference Errors**:
   - ○ **Error**: Using a variable before it is declared or defined.
   - ○ **Fix**: Ensure that variables are declared before use.
   - ○ **Example Fix**:

```
let y = 10;
console.log(y); // Correct
console.log(z); // Incorrect
```

3. **Type Errors**:
   - ○ **Error**: Trying to call a method on an undefined or null value.
   - ○ **Fix**: Ensure that variables or objects are properly initialized before calling their methods.
   - ○ **Example Fix**:

```
let name = "John";
console.log(name.toUpperCase()); // Correct
let name = null;
console.log(name.toUpperCase()); // Incorrect
```

3. Recommended Tools and Resources for Web Development

Having the right tools can significantly improve productivity and efficiency in web development. Below are some essential tools and resources for developers:

1. Text Editors/IDE (Integrated Development Environment)

- **Visual Studio Code**: A powerful and popular text editor that supports extensions for HTML, CSS, JavaScript, and more.
- **Sublime Text**: A lightweight text editor known for its speed and simplicity.
- **Atom**: An open-source editor with a customizable interface and strong community support.
- **WebStorm**: A comprehensive IDE for JavaScript, HTML, and CSS with integrated support for debugging, testing, and version control.

2. Version Control Systems

- **Git**: A distributed version control system that allows developers to manage changes and collaborate effectively.
- **GitHub**: A platform for hosting Git repositories and collaborating with others on projects.
- **GitLab**: Another Git repository hosting service with integrated CI/CD (Continuous Integration/Continuous Delivery) features.

3. Debugging and Testing Tools

- **Chrome Developer Tools**: A suite of tools built into Google Chrome that help you inspect HTML, CSS, and JavaScript code, debug, and profile performance.
- **Firebug**: A popular Firefox extension for web development and debugging.
- **Jest**: A JavaScript testing framework for unit testing your code.
- **Selenium**: An automation tool for testing web applications.
- **Postman**: A tool for testing APIs by sending requests and viewing responses.

4. Frameworks and Libraries

- **React**: A JavaScript library for building user interfaces. It is component-based and helps create efficient, dynamic web applications.
- **Angular**: A platform and framework for building single-page client applications using HTML and TypeScript.
- **Vue.js**: A progressive JavaScript framework for building UIs and single-page applications.
- **Bootstrap**: A front-end framework for creating responsive and mobile-first web pages.
- **jQuery**: A JavaScript library that simplifies HTML document traversal and manipulation.

5. Responsive Design Tools

- **Browser Developer Tools**: Most modern browsers (Chrome, Firefox) have built-in developer tools that allow you to simulate different screen sizes and resolutions for responsive testing.
- **Figma/Adobe XD/Sketch**: Tools for designing and prototyping web layouts, including mobile and desktop versions, which can then be implemented using HTML, CSS, and JavaScript.

6. Online Learning Platforms

- **freeCodeCamp**: Offers free coding tutorials for HTML, CSS, JavaScript, and more.
- **MDN Web Docs**: Provides comprehensive, up-to-date documentation on web technologies.
- **Coursera**: Offers courses on web development from universities and companies like Google.
- **Udemy**: A marketplace for learning, with a vast number of web development courses.

7. Online Communities

- **Stack Overflow**: A question-and-answer community for developers.
- **GitHub**: A platform where you can share code, collaborate on projects, and contribute to open-source projects.
- **Dev.to**: A social platform for developers to share articles, tutorials, and experiences.

By utilizing these tools and resources, you can streamline your development process, improve the quality of your code, and stay updated with industry trends.